I0811042

New & Selected Poems

of

Sarah Klassen

LYRIK POETRY SERIES 1

Series Editor: Nathan Dueck

New & Selected Poems

of

Sarah Klassen

Edited and with an introduction
by Nathan Dueck

CMU PRESS
WINNIPEG, MANITOBA
2024

CMU PRESS

CMU Press
Canadian Mennonite University
500 Shaftesbury Blvd.
Winnipeg MB R3P2N2
www.cmupress.ca

All rights reserved. No part of this publication may be reproduced in any form or by any means, electronic or mechanical, including photocopying, recording, or any information storage and retrieval system, without permission in writing from the publisher.

CMU Press is learning and striving to create an inclusive and welcoming space for people of many identities and communities. We work on land which is the ancestral home of the Anishinaabe, Cree, Dakota, and Métis peoples. We are grateful for their stewardship of this place.

The publication of this book has received financial support from the Katie Funk Wiebe Research Fund, administered by the Mennonite Brethren Historical Commission.

Series Editor: Nathan Dueck
Copyeditor: Sue Sorensen
Editorial assistance: Katie Doke Sawatzky, Felipio Abrenica, Phil Waldner
Cover and interior design: Jonathan Dyck

Printed in Canada by Friesens Corporation, Altona, Manitoba.
ISBN: 978-1-987986-13-6

Library and Archives Canada Cataloguing in Publication

Title: New & selected poems of Sarah Klassen / edited and with an introduction by Nathan Dueck.
Other titles: New and selected poems of Sarah Klassen
Names: Klassen, Sarah, 1932– author. | Dueck, Nathan, 1979– editor, writer of introduction.
Description: Series statement: Lyrik poetry series ; 1 | Includes bibliographical references and index.
Identifiers: Canadiana 20240362500 | ISBN 9781987986136 (softcover)
Subjects: LCGFT: Poetry.
Classification: LCC PS8571.L386 N49 2024 | DDC C811/.54—dc23

New poems and afterword © 2024 Sarah Klassen
Other poems © 1988, 1991, 1993, 1998, 1999, 2006
Copyright renewed 2024 Sarah Klassen.
Introduction Copyright © 2024 Nathan Dueck
Poems from *Monstrance* © 2012 Sarah Klassen, reprinted with permission, Turnstone Press (Winnipeg, MB). Poems from *The Tree of Life* © 2020 Sarah Klassen, reprinted with permission, Turnstone Press (Winnipeg, MB).

CONTENTS

Introduction

Nathan Dueck

It is hard not to think of Sarah Klassen as family. And what I mean by "family" is perhaps the notion of extended family. Though I am resigned to write about Klassen in accordance with academic convention, I must acknowledge that doing so does not characterize the relationship she develops with this reader—or, I argue, her audience in general. There is simply no way that Klassen expects us to button our Sunday-best or assign a grade to her composition. It is more like she is inviting readers into her care.

Sarah Klassen has a fine ear, and her poetry resounds with voices, mostly of women, that have not often appeared on the page—a grandmother speaking of how she came to Canada, a teacher talking about how language works (or fails to), a mother telling what a character from a story in the Bible means to her. That is not to say Klassen acts like a ventriloquist. If we want to think of her work in terms of performance, Klassen is more of a vocalist with dynamic range. Her poems appear to be the result of listening, an act of attentiveness, along with reflection, an act of interpretation that yearns to understand, but not make assumptions about, the story told. The idea, as many readers have pointed out, is that Klassen sensitively interprets both personal stories of adversities from the past and difficulties in the present. By presenting voices with clarity and control, Klassen prompts and occasionally even provokes us to listen to the still and small during an age of trumpets sounding.

AWARENESS

Klassen tends to write in a lyrical voice that strikes my ear as trustworthy. Without talking down to me, it appears to have my best interests in mind. Although the speakers of Klassen's poems do not often lecture, I can find myself reaching for a pencil to take marginal notes. In an interview with writer Miriam Maust from 1993, Klassen articulates the aesthetic she strives for in a poem: "I think if somebody expresses something about the inner world or the outer world in a fresh way and shows a dynamic use of language that draws the reader in (it's got to be interesting) that's part of it" (39). Poets, she proposes, are uniquely positioned among all writers to "explore the inner world with intelligence" by showing "how to use language, how to put it together, and how to work with images and say something" (Maust 39). I contend that Klassen demonstrates the depth of thought such an exploration demands. More specifically, she deploys precise diction and deliberate metaphor to evoke a sense of awareness.

Take, for example, the poem "Higher" from her most recent collection, *The Tree of Life* (2020). It opens with a quotation from third-century Christian theologian Origen—one that Klassen uses as an epigraph twice over her oeuvre—"*You yourself are even another little world / And have within you the sun and the moon / And also the stars.*" With those words, the speaker prepares the implied audience to "Hunger for something more than bread" as "you rise up" to an internal plane where "solitude will be your soul companion." That play on words, soul for sole, signals that the poem's subject is simultaneously spiritual and personal. The speaker then implores us to "Listen to your own breathing, / give ear to the alarm within: a congregation, a quarreling crowd / of shoppers, a kindergarten class." The purpose of paying attention thus is to notice "The whole world sits at the centre of your self, / waiting to be loved, forgiven, reconciled." If we can perceive that profound depth within ourselves, we might prepare ourselves to recognize its presence inside someone else. The urgency of that state of mind, recalling the philosophy of Simone Weil—especially in *Simone Weil: Songs of Hunger and Love* (1999)—informs so much of Klassen's oeuvre.

In a "Tribute to Sarah Klassen" from 2008, critic of Mennonite literature Hildi Froese Tiessen offers this generous overview:

> Sarah Klassen [has] often invoked, with sensitivity, insight, and grace, the environment and sensibilities of people who had gone before. In a goodly number of her poems she records compelling personal memories—memories she has assembled from others, as well as her own—and, by force of her wonderful poetic voice, she transcribes the past and inscribes it with a palpable force of emotion. (94)

I would add that by scripting memories that way, Klassen exhibits an important function of empathy. Paying close attention as she does can develop the "sensitivity, insight, and grace" that Tiessen describes. Moreover, Klassen indicates that such self-awareness is not an end in and of itself. We must also take care to become aware of our limitations. By that, Klassen urges us to see beyond conventional or traditional patterns of thought. She calls attention to beliefs that heal the body and others that harm it, along with those behaviours that unite the body politic and the arguments that divide it. For Klassen, the truth of recorded history may be doubtful and the quality of received wisdom is sometimes questionable, but the value of becoming aware is eternal. That is how she presents lived-in moments without slipping into mundanity. Similarly, the anecdotes she presents resist seeming routine.

SENSITIVITY

To my mind, the most affecting aspect of Klassen's poetry is its depiction of suffering. I suspect this "affect" results from her engagement with concepts Mennonites are generally preoccupied with: insecurity about religious ethics, redemption of hard work, and difficulty of independence. The poem "Collector" from Klassen's first collection, *Journey to Yalta* (1988), renders those thematic concerns with remarkable sensitivity. It begins with a stunning statement, "My mother throws nothing away." With the next two lines, the speaker personifies mother by focusing on a skill she accrued over a lifetime: "She has fingers fashioned to gather / small hard seed from fruit that's over-ripe." The next few lines list the contents of mother's collection, which could imply that the clutter of bric-a-brac and curios is how mother marks time. However, the poem complicates such an interpretation. It would appear mother retains these items because "she's had to abandon too much /

in Russia" when her family fled. The subsequent list is far weightier than the first, including "Scent of apricot blossoms," "the green silk dress her mother made," and "Friends / and the graves of sisters." Mother must have curated that collection of miscellany in reaction to deep-seated suffering. In response, the speaker demonstrates care for mother by annotating the collection with compassion. Before leaving her village, mother remembers uttering "Furtive last words, prayers spoken / embracing the train's shadow." In the speaker's telling, belief in God offered some comfort, but it did not prevent the past from pursuing mother throughout her life.

Even though I have read "Collector" many times, the poem still makes the hair on my forearms rise. To come to terms with that reaction, I must briefly consult French philosophers Gilles Deleuze and Felix Guattari's definition of "affect" in *A Thousand Plateaus*: "Affects are becomings" (256). In the notes to his translation of that text, Brian Massumi glosses "L'affect" as "a prepersonal intensity corresponding to the passage from one experiential state of the body to another and implying an augmentation or diminution in that body's capacity to act" (xvi). In other words, an affect is a reaction that occurs prior to or apart from thought. Massumi distinguishes affect from emotion in his influential essay "The Autonomy of Affect." He draws on Spinoza to demonstrate "the irreducibly bodily and autonomic nature of affect" (Massumi, "Affect" 28). Whereas emotion results from conscious interpretation, affect is largely unconscious. In "The Turn to Affect: A Critique," Ruth Leys takes issue with "the belief that affect is independent of signification and meaning" (443). She addresses the literary type of affect in a note about "affective reactions": "The fact that a novel or painting makes me feel or think a certain way may be a significant aspect of my response to the work, but, simply as my response, it has no standing as interpretation of it" (451). By contrasting "affect" and "form, cognition, and meaning," Leys suggests that readers engage with aesthetics (450). Presumably, readers contact or connect with a text by experiencing an "asignifying intensity" (Massumi, "Autonomy" 31) prior to making meaning.

Dwelling on affect may appear to be a ploy to explain away my reaction to "Collector." But there is no denying that even when I reread the poem a shudder of intensity passes between me and it. In truth, I suddenly feel the urge to call my own grandmother, because she arrived in Canada at about the same time as the mother from "Collector." In this poem, Klassen catalogues a few items that relate to the suffering her mother endured prior to immigration. She does so by engaging an aesthetic that writer and editor Maurice Mierau astutely terms the "Mennonite sensibility" (77). Employing Mierau's definition, much of Klassen's poetry "includes some intellectual or visceral knowledge of Mennonite experience (preferably both), whether that experience be cultural, historical, theological or literary (preferably all of these)" (77–78). With the exception of *Simone Weil: Songs of Hunger and Love*, each of Klassen's collections includes poems about family and other stories of Mennonite experience. And, according to Mierau, one reason for "making art out of one's own experience and history" is to illustrate how "that history is different from the official version of propaganda and pulpit" (71). With her work, Klassen negotiates that difference with compassion, which explains her place of respect within Mennonite letters.

While a Mennonite sensibility informs the poetry Klassen composes about her family, it is worth noting that her concerns range outside the community as well. In fact, I would adjust Mireau's formulation to propose that Klassen's poetry is also informed by a Mennonite *sensitivity*. Whether Klassen writes about educating high schoolers, exploring the Interlake, or explicating Bible stories, she addresses these subjects with specific "cultural, historical, theological or literary" insight. By that I mean she is interested in understanding the ethical response to human suffering. At the end of her interview with Klassen, Maust comments about the prevalence of imagery in *Journey to Yalta* that illustrates "how frangible, yet how tough, humans are" (44). Klassen replies that she is curious to know about the ways people recover from harm and about "our constant quest for healing" (45). She explains that healing can take place in "the body or spirit or mind or soul," but there is no guarantee that it will happen: "You don't always find that healing—but there's always that quest, that journey for healing" (45). Healing, then, provides hope to overcome the borders built to deny Lithuanian independence (as in *Borderwatch*, 1993) and the violence in Ukraine during and following the Russian Revolution (as in *Violence and Mercy*, 1991). It offers peace to sixteenth-century Anabaptist heretics and a seventeenth-century Dutch engraver (as in *Dangerous Elements*, 1998). It even gives grace to meddlesome birds (as in *Monstrance*, 2012) and misshapen trees (as in *The Tree of Life*).

HANDS, ROSES, AND STONES

Recurring motifs of hands, roses, and stones appear prominently in Klassen's poetry. In fact, I like to think of them as providing something of a Rosetta Stone, revealing what we should pay some attention to. Deciphering how they function is key to understanding Klassen's thoughts about women, memory, and spirituality, so I will offer a few samples below.

Throughout Klassen's poetry, hands tend to represent the work that women do. They make their first appearance in "Small Deaths," the first poem of *Journey to Yalta*, as the speaker describes ongoing familial grief:

> Too often my Grandmother buried
> her babies. Their spirits slipped from her
> hands like startled birds
> or wayward angels no one can persuade
> to stay.

Klassen returns to the same image in "Moving On" from *Borderwatch* when grandmother sits motionless with "her hands like stone in her lap / which had borne eight children." Here, she associates hands with a nurturing mother. Furthermore, she builds on to the idea a simile that suggests grandmother is the foundation of her family structure. Klassen places mother in the role of Eve caring for an Edenic garden in "Genesis" from *A Curious Beatitude*: "Her fingers crave the warmth of summer earth. / Crave rain." Alternately, Klassen uses mother's hands in "Blue Chair" from *Dangerous Elements* to ponder why God would permit pain to enter our bodies as we age.

There are several instances in Klassen's poetry where hands appear next to roses. "Warning to Residents" from *Borderwatch* provides an affecting example. The poem takes the form of an unsigned letter posted at a convalescent home. The anonymous author asks readers to resist the heart-rending pleas from an elderly woman "who comes to you with outstretched hands / begging for bread / water." Later, however, readers are also told to request stories from that resident "about the apples / and the white rose." The poem does not explain the image, leaving us to wonder just what about those tales is notable—specifically, why is the rose white? Because we cannot question the elderly woman, we are left to empathize on our own.

For Klassen, roses seem to represent memories that are difficult to deal with. Some of those memories are worth keeping, but a few we could do without. "today," a poem from *Dangerous Elements*, begins with a simile where the speaker yearns to be free from the past:

i will live quite simply
as if the hand's clenched fingers
could be persuaded to let go
open like petals of a rose

Roses can also suggest a historical transition, like a change in season. "Agenda" from *Journey to Yalta* ends with the speaker "wrap[ping] gunny sacks around rose bushes" to "brace for winter." In *A Curious Beatitude*, the speaker of "Rewinding Time" again covers "rose bushes with burlap" after attending father's funeral. But roses can also represent small kindnesses, as when the speaker in "Cataract" (from *Journey to Yalta*) brings mother "blood-red roses," along with a radio, before her surgery.

Klassen is also drawn to the contrast between roses and stones. In "Triptych," from *Borderwatch*, the speaker offers three snapshots of Lithuania in tercets. In the first section, a visit to the market results in "The roses you desire" just as long as they are "white. Unopened. In odd numbers" in order "to escape death." That superstition pairs with the belief that Christ emerges "carved from hard-grained oak," "beside stone walls," and "at a roadside / grown familiar." Klassen describes Lithuania's capital, Vilnius, with comparable imagery in "Guide to the KGB Museum" from *Monstrance*.

In general, stones in Klassen's poetry imply a spiritual presence. Unsurprisingly, they surface in poems about contemplation or meditation. In *Journey to Yalta*, the speaker of "Haggai" starts with the assertion "There is no poetry in Haggai" before prophesying about the importance of rebuilding the temple in Jerusalem:

Heaving stones, pounding them
into place, under cleaving heat
of the sun, climbing the steep slopes
to the cedars, hewing pillars
for our God.

The voice in "On the Banks of the Nile" from *Violence and Mercy* likely belongs to the prophet Jeremiah, given that the poem addresses "fugitives from Judah" with the promise "All things begin and end / with words." The implied audience must pay attention because "The ones you speak are heavy / as stone," so "They won't ring out / or echo back from the slant sides / of pyramids." With that simile, the exiled Judeans are reminded that language itself provides a kind of home. In *Monstrance*, "The Race" directs audiences to the book of Revelation, where God's word "ends in metaphor." For the record, in an essay from 1998 entitled "Faith, Art, and Reconciliation," Klassen recognizes "the Bible's way of telling truth through story and song, image and vision," or, in other words, metaphor. Those "concrete means" of artistic imagination "reach the heart through the body." That is why, in Klassen's telling, holy scripture is everything but straightforward. The speaker reports "Your new name [will be] plainly carved / in white stone," and then mentions "The promised morning star." Presumably, the heavenly body of that last line is Christ, and one day He will call roll.

Tempted as I am to delve into the symbology of bread or silence, for example, in Klassen's poetry, it behooves me to describe the arrangement of this current selection of her poems into eight sections. The title of each section comes from a poem therein that signals its theme. Instead of listing a selection of poems chronologically, I assembled poems in an order that I felt represented ideas and imagery Klassen turns and returns to. What follows is a brief synopsis of each section along with a reading of the poem that provides its title.

Rewinding Time

The first section contains Klassen's poetry about her family's emigration from the Russian steppe. With these poems about parents and grandparents, Klassen traces the steps of her ancestors from *Journey to Yalta* to *Monstrance*. The poem "Rewinding Time," for example, is an elegy that reflects on Thomas Hardy's "The Darkling Thrush." In that poem, the tiny titular bird releases a song that awakens hope in listeners who feel hardened by "Winter's dregs." Approximately a century later, "Rewinding Time" invokes Hardy's lines to illustrate the life of "our father" who did not live until the millennium's end. With the image of "The Century's corpse outleant," Hardy asserts that the nineteenth century must pass to make way for the twentieth century. Klassen responds by indicating that the surviving family in her own time must fill in for a father who has fallen silent. Movement is a dual motif in "Rewinding Time," illustrating how father migrated to Western Canada, and how he performed music as he matured into adulthood. While father "made displays for Eatons" and constructed "miniature cultivators, John Deere tractors, plows . . . from scraps," his family proceeds into "The future imminent." The poem ends by acknowledging that movement is unending. A final image contrasts the speed at which time passes on a rotating earth with the near permanence of celestial beings hurtling through their individual orbits.

Artist and Medium

Visual art often inspires Klassen's poetry. The resulting ekphrastic poems additionally can be meditations about the expressive capacity of language. For example, several engravings by Dutch artist Jan Luyken (1649-1712) inform a suite of poems in *Dangerous Elements*. In one of them, "Artist and Medium," Klassen imagines the process Luyken underwent when etching scenes in copper of Mennonite torture victims, for publication in *Martyrs Mirror*. Contending that "Jan Luyken finds no words for it [martyrdom]," Klassen provides an impressive few of her own. The poem juxtaposes the "agony and exultation" of making art with the "triumphant dying" for the cause of religion. The crux, though, involves the proper method for depicting faith: "should it be modest or bold, / reasonable, fervent, fanatical?" After mulling the morality of his aesthetics, Luyken choses "the plain" and "the raw." Klassen ends the poem with a beatific gesture of "the impatient soul" who is striving "ecstatically for God." I must admit that I was not raised in a home with *Martyrs Mirror* next to the family Bible on the mantel, so Klassen's poetry introduced me to the existence of Luyken's tome while simultaneously informing me about its importance.

A Matter of Language

Klassen was well established in her teaching career when she began writing poetry. So, of course, many of her most absorbing poems are about the classroom. In her work from *Borderwatch* and *Violence and Mercy*, Klassen carefully considers what education means, and occasionally scrutinizes how language itself functions. And her words are weighty; hard lessons may be necessary for maturity. "A Matter of Language," for example, is an apostrophe whereby the speaker addresses an audience seated in desks:

> Your being here
> (and mine)
> has everything to do
> with language

The speaker is a teacher whose pedagogy does not begin and end with the textbook. This lesson is about how "to articulate affliction." Soon, the distance between the "opposite sides / of the desk" collapses as teacher and pupils both try to come to terms with a "violent / border incident." The truth, the teacher concludes, is that "Language / or lack of it / can not protect flesh." With those words, Klassen indicates that while education can communicate knowledge, wisdom comes with awareness of what one does not know.

Colours at the Border

Over the course of her career, Klassen occasionally taught the English language to students and teachers in former Soviet states. The poems about her travels in *Borderwatch* and *Dangerous Elements* serve as a lyrical and spiritual travelogue. Klassen's thesis, if it is fair to say there is an overarching argument in these poems, is that students are students no matter where they learn, but what distinguishes them is what they must learn about. For example, "Colours at the Border" asks readers to perceive a geographical boundary as unnatural. The first statement of the poem, "Absence of colour at the border / is not neutrality," proposes that there are political consequences to every action. In other words, we must not fool ourselves to believe anyone can hide behind "dull / camouflage" or disappear within "a uniform state of mind." Following the status quo equates to "Stubborn reluctance ever to say yes / to radiance." Reading this poem in context, the speaker refers to the border separating Lithuania from Poland, where the red poppy is the national flower. So, when that voice describes "poppies, blood-red" and "green fields," the poem's title becomes literal. Those colours appear on both sides of the border. The landscape refuses to recognize any sort of artificially imposed division.

Still Life with Light

Every now and then one of Klassen's poems reads very much like a journal entry. (Perhaps I should have added "that you can read without feeling guilty about it" at the end of the previous sentence.) In this category of poetry, peppered throughout every collection, Klassen writes about surveying her surroundings until something definitively catches her eye. Imagery of prairie flora and fauna flourish in these diaristic poems. But Klassen is just as eager to take in domestic life as she is gazing out at the natural world through a picture window. For example, as its title would suggest, "Still Life with Light" has a light tone. It begins with alliteration of plosive *p* and glottal *o* sounds to present the pleasant experience of "Peeling an orange this morning / and planning lunch." The speaker reflects on that work with lilting liquid *l*'s: "there's nothing lovely / as light on still life." As the poem luxuriates in "pure / morning turning the muted background / bright," readers may revel in the nasal *m*'s and bilabial *b*'s. After a sumptuous lunch with friends, the speaker anticipates "We'll sip our coffee / until someone rises" and "the rest of us" enjoy grazing on fruit "or just sitting / still." With those words, Klassen reminds us to pay attention to the moment and ask ourselves whether we are rising to meet it.

Alpha and Omega

It is not necessary to attend catechism classes to know the Bible is a complicated book. That may be why I appreciate the poems where Klassen interprets a story from holy scripture. From her first collection to her last, she has been drawn to the Jewish Bible, which is noteworthy for a Mennonite writer. I want to crack wise that Klassen must arrive at church on time, since she has obviously heard the Old Testament readings, but such a joke only emphasizes the depth of her faith. It is as though she has a curated a canon of her own. Either that, or she has offered a thorough commentary. For example, in the poem "Alpha and Omega," Klassen represents creation in a manner that would make even Gerard Manley Hopkins nod in approval. Although she is not quite writing sprung rhythm, a line like "Let fish rejoice in it fantastically, the fur of fox, cat, cougar, / coyote be haloed" bounces around the tongue reading it aloud. In fact, the rhythm of the poem, which begins with strict iambs, eventually metamorphizes like the creation it describes. The poem loosely follows the pattern of creation in the first chapter of Genesis, and when humanity appears in the evidence of civilization—"breakfast bowls" and "empty cups" are filled with the light of dawn—the syllables are strewn about, stressed and unstressed. At the ending, though, when the speaker directly addresses "O light of life," the rhythm regains order: "You melt the iron grip of fear. The stone-cold, / guarded grave can never hold you." I cannot settle on whether to write "amen" or "selah" to this, so I will conclude with both.

Pensées

In a conceptual departure, Klassen channels the voice of Simone Weil for her collection *Simone Weil: Songs of Hunger and Love*. Although she had written from another's perspective in many other poems, Klassen had not previously taken on a persona at such length. This exploration of the mysticism and politics of the French philosopher speaks to Klassen's thematic interests: the unknowability of God, the intricacies of communicating between generations, and the prevalence of violence in the modern world. Weil's idea of insatiable desire also intrigues Klassen. In a form of self-abnegation, Weil denied herself food. The necessity of sacrifice is a theme in Klassen's poems. In her incisive and, frankly, inspiring essay from 2010, "Hunger, History, and the 'Shape of Awkward Questions': Reading Sarah Klassen's Simone Weil as Mennonite Text," writer and scholar Tanis MacDonald argues

> Klassen uses her Mennonite sensibility to ask questions through Weil and of Weil, a historical figure whose "obstinate refusal" to compromise on the rigor of her beliefs and practices of austerity had a Mennonite sensibility of its own. (89)

It is worth noting that according to Weil, only God can create something from nothing, but humans can *de*create themselves by exchanging their free will for God's will. And that process, as MacDonald puts it, pits Weil's "insatiable spiritual hunger against her food austerities," through which Klassen determines that such "saintliness demands difficulty" (92). Within Weil's notion of hunger are a number of thematic possibilities that MacDonald relates to Mennonite literature. MacDonald's reasoning is more intricate than I can summarize here, so it will have to suffice to say that "the hunger for home is a spiritual hunger" (98). And the paradox of home and hunger compares with "The immigration of Mennonites to the rich arable soil of Southern Manitoba—land that is also perpetually subject to drought, flooding, pests, and hail" (MacDonald 98). And that concept of home, simultaneously illusory and elusive, aligns with Klassen's Mennonite sensitivity.

The poem "*Pensées*" explores that sort of contradiction. In Klassen's telling, Weil processes her relationship with the divine presence by providing paradoxical examples of what it is not. The poem provides analogies that move from abstract to concrete, considering how "imagination" cannot "fill the emptiness" and the way that "growth of wings" cannot "defy gravity." The poem proceeds to fragment as though fragments of thought pass through Weil's mind. And Klassen's careful use of line breaks leads audiences to muse on possible interpretations. Weil contemplates Christ's "shroud of disbelief" during crucifixion as He "cries out *my God / my God*." The conclusion of the poem proposes a statement of theology, quoting the words of Weil: "*God exists because I desire him*." What is not clear is whether that is Weil articulating her own thoughts or thoughts she is attributing to Christ during crucifixion. The italics would seem to imply the latter, but there is no definitive interpretation. And that is where Klassen proves her sensitivity. Such a statement of empathy, however interpolated, demonstrates her understanding of suffering.

Heimatlied

Often the subject of Klassen's poems, both the speaker and implied audience, is a woman. Klassen conveys the most significant moments in the life of that woman, young and old, public and private. These poems rely on anecdote to tell moving stories of pain and endurance. For example, "*Heimatlied*" from

Borderwatch depicts the perspective of an elderly woman who "speaks frequently / of going home." The voice of the poem clarifies that by home "She doesn't mean / the white bungalow on some suburban street," "the shack / sheltered by green aspen," or "the solid brick / house abandoned in the village / Vassilyevka." Instead, the old woman's

> Home
> is farther off than that.
> And nearer. It is neither north
> nor south. It is a far country
> carried in the heart.

Despite the title of the poem, home is not a "land" per se. Although I imagine the speaker here implies heaven, these "streets [are] / neither pointed stones nor gold." For the old woman, home lives in the "sweet / remembered stanzas of a song / she sings for you." Instead of a location bound to time and space, home is more like a hymn.

Even though we are not indeed family, the poetry that Sarah Klassen writes can touch me as though we were. But, when shivers spread across my skin while I read about grandmother, when my stomach knots while I read about travelling through Lithuania to teach English, or a breath catches in my throat when I recognize the behaviour of a Bible character, Klassen helps focus my thoughts and even calm my mind. She not only interprets suffering for her readers, but also displays the virtue of empathy. By paying attention the way Klassen does, we may develop a sensitivity to the voice crying in the wilderness.

Deleuze, Gilles, and Félix Guattari. *A Thousand Plateaus: Capitalism and Schizophrenia*. 1980. Translated by Brian Massumi, U of Minnesota P, 1987.

Klassen, Sarah. "Faith, Art, and Reconciliation." *Direction: A Mennonite Brethren Forum*, vol. 27, no. 2, 1998. https://directionjournal.org/27/2/faith-art-and-reconciliation.html

Leys, Ruth. "The Turn to Affect: A Critique." *Critical Inquiry*, vol. 37, no. 5, 2011, pp. 434–472.

Massumi, Brian. "The Autonomy of Affect." *Cultural Critique*, vol. 31, 1995, pp. 83–109.

---. "Notes on the Translation and Acknowledgements." *A Thousand Plateaus: Capitalism and Schizophrenia*, by Gilles Deleuze and Félix Guattari, 1980. Translated by Massumi, U of Minnesota P, 1987, pp. xvi–xix.

Maust, Miriam. "An Interview with Sarah Klassen." *The New Quarterly*, vol. 13, no. 3, 1993, pp. 34–45.

MacDonald, Tanis. "Hunger, History, and the 'Shape of Awkward Questions': Reading Sarah Klassen's Simone Weil as Mennonite Text." *Journal of Mennonite Studies*, vol. 28, 2010, pp. 87–102.

Mireau, Maurice. "Why Rudy Wiebe is Not the Last Mennonite Writer." *Conrad Grebel Review*, vol. 22, no. 2, 2004, pp. 69–82.

Tiessen, Hildi Froese. "A Tribute to Sarah Klassen." *Conrad Grebel Review*, vol. 26, no. 1, 2008, pp. 93–96.

Rise and Go

Rise and Go

1.
A migrant, told by a Voice to rise and go
into untravelled territory, walks with his wife.
His servants and his animals surround him.
He has no son to wrap his arm around.
Night falls. If anyone should ask,
Who are you?
what could he possibly say?
He is far from home, has miles to go,
and does not know the destination.
He pitches his tent and waits for the dawn.

2.
A prisoner in a barren cell asks:
Who am I?
The answer, because death is near, is urgent.
Can years of practising peace, opposing evil, praising love,
ever be proof enough? He's been a good son,
a faithful lover, loves his country. Fellow prisoners
admire his stalwart step, his incredible composure.

But at night, his heart beats at the bars of his confinement;
he is nothing but a broken reed. His knees are weak,
he is sick unto death. He hears the hammer blows
of new construction. A chapel? A house? A gallows.
Before morning breaks he will rise and go,
naked and empty-handed,
to somewhere he has never travelled.

Higher

You yourself are even another little world
And have within you the sun and the moon
And also the stars.—ORIGEN

Hunger for something more than bread
drives you to rise up, rise higher
to where the air is thin as a newborn's cry,
the view unobstructed. At this height,
solitude will be your soul companion.
You ascend a mountain towering up from wilderness,
climb a ladder, shimmy up a pillar in the desert.
You are prepared to leave behind what you cannot carry
on your back or in your head. You cannot bring the children.
Keep both hands free: one to hold tight,
while reaching with the other for the next rung. Night falls;

silence surrounds you like a wall. Listen to your own breathing,
give ear to the alarm within: a congregation, a quarrelling crowd
of shoppers, a kindergarten class. Wisdom vies with triviality,
doubt with trust. Rage wants to outshout praise.
Are you surprised that you hauled up with you to this altitude
a multitude? The whole world sits at the centre of your self,
waiting to be loved, forgiven, reconciled.
Morning comes. Sun rises.
The desert wind blows sand into your eyes.

And yet

The city of refuge is burning.
Smoke and panic fill the air.
Someone says: *Let not your hearts be troubled.*

Words easily spoken. A mantra
to quiet the quaking heart.
A line of poetry.

Fear makes things fall apart.
Knees like water; the heart troubled.
Even a prophet questions the chances.

And yet—beside the brook, the ravens.
And yet—the widow
and the widow's son.

> *Don't be afraid,* the prophet dares to say.
> *Dip into the flour. Tip the jug of oil.*
> *Bake bread as usual.*

Travelling with children
Or: Sermon series in a Mennonite church

1.

During our weeks with Moses, we made bricks with straw,
bore the burden of tough quotas,
shrank from each lacerating whiplash.
At night, we listened to the keening of women
who had given birth. We dreamt a saviour
would come and tear us free.

Then we escaped,
thanks to Moses, Aaron, and of course, God.
Miriam composed the praise we loved to sing
sun up, sun down. After the pastoral prayer,
the weekly offering, we compared notes:
which of the plagues had been most cruel,
which most apt, which pharaoh
had we most feared, most hated, wanted dead?

One question troubled us:
Who is this God not one of us has ever actually seen?
Whose hand snatched us from slavery?
Whose voice called us from the river, led us
with flame and fog through wilderness, and left us
bewildered?

2.

Light poured that morning through stained glass.
Rainbow colours fell on us like jewels.
We were told to claim clothes from the closets
of terrified neighbours who said:
Take! Take your unleavened bread and go
just go!

In the parking lot we debated: lunch at Perkins or Olive Garden?
We marvelled at Divinity's mysterious ways.
How rich we had become.
Never mind our children's restlessness,
the sun's relentless hammering, dry distances
we'd have to plod between departure and arrival,
bearing the weight of plunder.

How quickly in that wilderness
we all grew weary of manna.

3.

Once you've lived beside a river,
you'll always want to rest your burning eyes
on water. Your sore feet crave
immersion in cool currents.

Thirst became our nourishment. Our children,
bored sitting too long under another gush of words,
begged to be released. Sometimes we said yes.
Sometimes we followed them down the aisle
to find a fountain.

It wasn't long before we longed for that river.
We wanted to unsay complaints spoken on its banks.
Confessions stuck to our parched throats, our tongues
too thick with thirst.

We looked for a stream not yet gone dry,
a pool, a puddle. We stopped insisting it must be un-
contaminated, deep enough for immersion.
No one expected to walk on water. Only that it should moisten
the burning lips of our children.

4.

Sunday after Sunday we were at the mercy
of a company of preachers, ordained or lay,
male or female, old, young, educated,
or not so much. All of them
instructing us to set up or collapse
our weathered tents. In that blazing desert
we packed and repacked our possessions,
rounded up our grumbling children.

We wanted an end to wandering. An end to head counts.
We wanted the landscape altered, the sky crammed
with clouds able to deliver rain. We wanted
water running clear through unfrozen pipes,
rust-free, colourless, abundant.

The morning Moses split the rock
we were shocked,
as if in the midst of a church picnic
the heavens opened. That fierce gush
caught us off guard. We expected a hymn.
Announcements. The benediction.

Our children opened their parched mouths
and drank.

5.

One morning, the burning bush became the children's story,
their chance to face the sacred. Our chance to watch their faces
glow as the fire blazed, consuming nothing.
Take off your shoes, we said, and they did.

Trapped in that desert we learned that fire,
when it is hot enough, will melt gold.
Out of gold we reconfigured God.

When Moses climbed down (finally) from the mountain,
his face blazed. We raised our hands
to shield the faces of our children,
then covered our own.

Rewinding Time

Small deaths

Too often my Grandmother buried
her babies. Their spirits slipped from her
hands like startled birds
or wayward angels no one can persuade
to stay.

Before she could call out
or close her thin fingers, their eyes
fell shut. Someone placed them in lace-
lined boxes, pinned pink roses
to the folds of their white sleeves.

Two survived. My mother
and her younger brother left
unfinished quarrels long enough
to consider the stilled lashes
the small white feet
pointing forever to the sky.

Grandmother, grieving
searched all conceivable corners
of her soul
for evidence of unexamined sin.

Grandfather
who always called the doctor
too late, sits upright beside a small coffin
hands splayed on his knees. Mouth tight.
His eyes bright nails that hold together
life and death.

Year after year
he stares straight past me

facing unafraid
the omniscient eye of God who is merciful.
Who is just.

Preparation

Having nothing
more to lose
Grandfather
forged a footstool
three-legged
solid
for the long journey to Yalta.

Hammer blows
driving nails deep
into silence
sandpaper
rasping on wood.

All afternoon
fragments of birdsong
weaving his heart's heaviness
in and out of
soft spring wind.

He didn't speak
to his children
about fear and loss.
Labourers unwilling
to tip their hats to
Ivan Petrovich.
Knives, hoofbeats
imagined and real.

He only told them
it's farther than you think
from Barvenkovo
to the Black Sea.

A long way for your mother
sitting on the hard floor of a cattle car.

Barvenkovo, 1918

After the revolution silkworms
appear in the village. Women
arrange them on oak tables overlaid
with mulberry branches.

Silkworms need no invitation
to feed. Night and day
they dig in greedy, gorge themselves
on splayed foliage.

Cocooned
they are immersed
by the wondering women
in water, a kind of warm death
then unspun slowly
threads pulled fine
from their centres, a revolution
in reverse.

Twirling
the homemade spools
the women, repelled less by worms
than by wounds and the cruel shape
of violence (before the revolution
rare as these worms) can't imagine
how they will fashion
a whole fabric
their work-worn fingers, needles flying
from the singular unravelling
of this death.

Treatment

Grandmother
neither cringed
nor cried out
when Russian doctors collapsed
her left lung.

She never expected
healing
to come easy.

Each evening after sundown
the long needle
forced between ribs, a violation
she accepted. She understood

the need for wounds
and blood.
The complete terror
of descending darkness
lifted
before one can breathe
easy
again.

Collector

My mother throws nothing away.
She has fingers fashioned to gather
small hard seed from fruit that's over-ripe
hold it a while in her closed hands
and hide it from the wind.

Everything adheres to her.
Last year's calendars, lacy patterns
for crochet, pineapple and pinwheel
weeks of yellow bulletins
saved from the Brethren church, envelopes
bills were mailed in.
She collects them with her whole heart.

Keeps newspaper pictures of kings
and queens in boxes under her bed.
They are posed smiling from balconies
on wet moors walking their dogs
or waving sadly from a yacht in Yalta.

She tells me she's had to abandon too much
in Russia. Scent of apricot blossoms
in April, the green silk dress her mother made
shade of a twisted oak, rough-branched, rooted
beside rivers. Friends
and the graves of sisters.

The leaving was hushed
and final. Furtive last words, prayers spoken
embracing the train's shadow. She tells me
how full their hearts were of fear
and emptiness, how they breathed
the last thin smoke from the village.

How little they could carry
in their clasped hands.

Genesis

Our mother planted her prairie garden in March,
covered the shriveled seeds with soil and watered them.
Before we knew it east windows burgeoned
with green pepper sprouts, parsley, tiny tomatoes.
We watched with ravenous hope. In March

my gardening friend turns her back to the blizzard
in the window, snowman grinning from the storm-
bound yard. She's curled on the couch, lost in glossy
Homes and Gardens, stuck between seductive pages
of seed catalogues. She's driving winter out with visions
of plump tulips, the first blue crocus breaking through.
Her fingers crave the warmth of summer earth.
Crave rain.

I'm skiing through a birdless wood, my head filled up
with gardens, gliding past aspen and oak, hawthorn
and barren birch, dreaming their empty branches green.
Dreaming this wintry world a tangle of lush vines, undergrowth
a person could get lost in. Orchids blooming pink and mauve.
The apple shining on a pristine tree. In its vicinity the serpent coils.
The carolling of newborn birds fills everything and everywhere
light (and the first thin shadow) shivers across the green.

Blue chair

My mother in her blue chair is afraid
she can't get up: knees gorged with pain,
wrists, ankles stiff as boards.
She's afraid
God's forgotten her. She wants to die.
Wants to walk once more between the rows of snap
dragons, pumpkins. I hate to mention the mud,
rabbits grazing the peas, the cat that got the rabbit.
She's forgotten the flood.
Asks me if I've seen a rainbow lately. No.

I'm arranging candles on a chocolate cake,
flexing my fingers, wrists, testing for evidence:
a hint of pain, stiffness, a latent legacy.
She's ninety now. Her brother (five years younger,
his memory excellent, body strong)
reads Psalm 90: *God*
you have been our dwelling place. He reads:

A thousand years are like a dream.
How quickly grass fades,
and winter's here. All water frozen over,
garden and the shivering rabbits white.
My mother dozing in her blue chair dreams
gardens in another country
a half-remembered revolution, the last
thin residue of light.

Moving on

Grandmother in old age
allowed her sons to carry her
up steep church steps to hear the preacher
speak about leaping and dancing.
She sat without moving
her hands like stone in her lap
which had borne eight children

the fourth just coming
when blood-red eddies of dust
explode the whole steppe. A blinding charge
of daggers cleaves the terrified air above the bed
where she lies writhing at each sharp thrust
of pain, not caring about the quantity of grain,
carriages, the best matched horses, land

                                        or even life itself.
When they lift her one last time
her granddaughters awkward in their adolescence
listen to the choir sing:

auf Adler's Fluegeln getragen
bis hinein in die Ewigkeit

The woman's hands are pale
wings folded on a black dress. The slack
cheeks white. The hair thin strands of grey
on a satin pillow. The appalling mystery of closed eyes.

The granddaughters imagine her eyelids flicker
open as if a great light touched them
and grandmother breathes amazed:

was kein Auge gesehen
und kein Ohr gehoert
und in keines Menschen Herz gekommen ist

Hearts beating, breathless, they wish for wings
or merciful boys on motor bikes
to fly them along the city's dust-choked streets
swiftly as eagles up to the wide highway,
wind and the engine's roar victorious in their ears.
Hair flung back. They desire

quick ignition.
A blinding explosion. A vision
of pure light.

Interlake childhood II

My father promised he'd be a farmer
if only they'd let him live
in Canada. He could never forget
promises. When the last snow vanished
from the bush, he resigned himself
to stubborn fields
he'd given his best years to clear
of poplar and oak.

Stones surfaced like white whales
from a black ocean. He watched mute
hawks divide the sky
into capricious patterns.
Scanning the west horizon
he learned to wait for rain.

When the Ford broke down
he tore its entrails out
a passionate evisceration
and laid the parts in lyrical patterns
on canvas. Spark plugs and shafts
and wires. I watched him
fields bleak bush forgotten
orchestrate with his earth-blackened
greasy fingers
in concert with the hum of insects
a summer symphony.

He lived those oil-stained hours with joy.
His heart sank like mine
when the sun fell past the horizon
a cruel interruption
of the day's play.

In translation

Und es rauschte als wollte es regnen.

I know what they mean, these words
my mother recited
when she heard the west wind
wrestling with poplars
and her garden needed rain.

The German word for *wind* is missing
from what she remembered
but is implied. Isn't it
obviously intended?

I wanted to write a poem that catches
the rasp of wind assaulting aspen,
whipping lake waves into turbulence,
white water slapping shoreline rocks.
A poem in two languages, one voice.

But how do I translate
rauschen into English?

The wind blows where it chooses.
You hear its high-pitched wail, its rising
crescendo, cringe from its cold fury,
its burning summer breath. When it abates
you say: it is dying down. Now

there is silence so startling
the poem is held suspended
in the satin air. Now
it needs no foreign or familiar words,
couldn't care less for the pleasure
of text in accurate translation.

Rewinding time

I leant upon a coppice gate
When Frost was spectre-gray,
And Winter's dregs made desolate
The weakening eye of day

...

The land's sharp features seem'd to be
The Century's corpse outleant,
His crypt the cloudy canopy,
The wind his death-lament.

—THOMAS HARDY, "THE DARKLING THRUSH"

Above us the pewter clouds and in the graveyard
geese hunkering near the pond, wind-milled, their eyes stiff
with indifference. They honk at us once or twice and won't budge.
It is Hardy's landscape: *The Century's corpse outleant.*

We have come to bury our father.
It could have been our brother, former colleague, a wife.

A story silenced.
An era gone for good. We wade through gold and grief.
Wind tears at our hair, our sombre overcoats and over there
that green carpet spread to camouflage a mound of earth.
A machine removed it, making room for the abandoned body.
This one has a mouth organ wedged between its *rigor mortis* fingers.
Another may have held a rose, a favourite cuddly bear, a book
crammed with mystery or news. Or nothing.

Over the closed casket
the preacher speaks in parables: wheat dropped into a black furrow
in spring.

But it's late fall.
We've raked our lawns for the last time this millennium, reeled in

stiff plastic hoses, harvested carrots, covered our lily bulbs
with mulch, rose bushes with burlap, emptied the eaves. How quickly
it's come round again to this. Just yesterday we watched the elm trees greening,
the neighbour's kid in water past the limits of his brand new rubber boots.

Yesterday that pretty bridge spanning the pond had not been built, the city
had not sprawled north, the father in this coffin had not learned to breathe,
pick out a tune on his harmonica. Had not discovered speech, reading,
the tangled skeins of love.

Someone leans over the coffin, a gesture repetition makes familiar:
pulling apart the fern, gerbera daises bright as the sun, lilies like cold snow.
You turn and walk away dismayed: how briefly anything that's beautiful,
that you most love, can last. Whole centuries of moments, days
scattered like petals.

                                        Goose droppings dot the yellow grass,
the flat bronze markers bearing beloved names. When we are gone
the machine will come, the last gold maple leaves will fall, snow
that before the cars speed off could cover everything.

                                        We will all,
some of us only once, some often, soon, come here again.

Coffee and fancy sandwiches. Uncommon leisure for retelling
a father's life. Those unfilled gaps in the beginning of the story.
A different country, an abandoned boy. If not for love
extended unexpectedly. . . . Isn't love always a surprise?
Home a hymn, a benediction?

                                        There was music in his blood
and planted in his brain hunger to fashion something new
from something old, hold in his restless agile hands
hammer and saw.

A ship crosses the ocean.
We push aside our cups, imagine a curl of smoke. An insignificant
dot on the horizon coming closer to the future
until the travellers at the railing spy the *land's sharp features.*
Gulls plummet and circle as we reel off alien names,
letting them slip familiar from our lips: Halifax harbour. Montreal.
Beechy, Saskatchewan. Niverville, Manitoba.
Clearbrook and Winnipeg.

Years of labour.
We say it and sigh while the grandkids brag:
Opa built Santa's village. It's true: he made displays for Eatons,
may have whistled while he worked, measured a tune, nailed
anger down, carved out a resolution to endure the course.
Fitting that the day he died the whole department store shut down.
And all the miniature cultivators, John Deere tractors, plows he made
from scraps with his retired hands. Used all of his allotted
three score years and ten and lived past eighty.

A minor player
in this almost spent millennium. Outshone by centuries of stars glittering
upon the stage, the playing field, the battle field, the information highway.
His structures and his songs eclipsed by new-found laws of relativity
and probability, quantum physics, mystery of DNA.
New planets added in his lifetime.

We become silent.
Now it's *the weakening eye of day.* Night closing in.
The millennium's *corpse outleant.*
A father buried.

The future imminent,
who'd want to chronicle ten centuries of floods, the lethal shifting
of tectonic plates, shocking tsunami. Year after year drought's devastation.
Wars, rumours of war, continents gorged on plague, genocide and waste.
And always some fanatic with his finger on the trigger.

But each *Brief History of Time* that sets down an expanding,
savage universe, has also this: springtime and harvest, snow and rain
and that warm stirring in the earth. A rainbow after supper
in the east. Comets we stayed awake to gape at, curious or terrified,
in every century, in heat or frost.

Remember
how we lay at midnight on the dock our father built, dizzy
watching the summer meteor showers? Radiance
that streaked across the utter dark reflected in the lake.
Satellites in silent progress through the solar system.
Our faces heavenward, stars in our eyes, we all believed
that we were falling,
falling into sky.

And always wind and sun contending
without end as if all living were a fable.

Which story and what star guided us?
Was there a *darkling thrush* warbling some *blessed Hope*
we scarcely heard or were completely unaware of?

Like Lear we stumble, blind and foolish, through the wilderness
mourning our wayward children. Or straddle tragedy like Ben
Heppner singing Tristan on TV. The tenor rising like a newborn star
before Isolde dies.

Before he died, our father
told us, by heart, stories of another country. Spoke of going home.
He didn't mean the wind-whipped shack in Beechy,
farm house in Niverville, the white suburban bungalow in Winnipeg.
And not that unexpected home across the ocean. Nor was this planet,
in his mind, his only home.

The pewter clouds have opened up a slit to let light through:
blood dappling the sullen sky. The coffee's cold. In future as in past
the wind blows where it chooses. We also must go home.
We are waiting for the snow, another camouflage. For music to ring out
the old, summon the new. As if our father's hand had once again
raised the harmonica, his warm lips breathed a new song into it.

Cataract

Besides these blood-red roses
I have brought you
a radio. I smuggled it
past clinical conspiracies
concealed in charts
and long white corridors.
Even tangled networks of plastic
tubes could not prevent me.

I am determined to keep you
in touch with the world.
Somewhere in Ethiopia
people are dying. Somewhere
fire swallows whole forests
valleys still smouldering
in spite of rain.

All this may not explain
my fear riding up the elevator
not knowing what to say.
After surgery your eyes bandaged
a white blankness meeting mine.

This radio will sing for you
waves rippling from warm lakes
laughter spilling like rain
on wet grain fields
a skyful of birdsong.

You must tune it right.
Uncontrolled these airwaves
swell with the rage of wind
whipped into storm

or the fierce roar of rivers
tumbling headlong
blindly
from rocks.

Procedure

1.
The doctor will sew live tissue
with delicate precision
into your right eye.
This requires fifteen stitches
one quarter of a hair's thickness,
fine needles, a microscope
and several priceless hours
of her time.

She will be gowned in green
scrubbed and gloved, a white sterile mask
pulled over her face.
You will be too numb to notice the colour
of her excellent eyes.

                    The live tissue
may be acquired by accident
or suicide. It is translucent, very small
and quivering like jelly. You must pray
it will become one easily
with your flesh.

They will not put you to sleep
completely. You may hear the faint scrape
of an instrument against the tray
purring of machines
the doctor's monotonous breathing. And voices

saying everything is well,
the needle moving in and out
on schedule.

You will lie there
wanting to blink your eyes. Try not to
make fists of your hands
or scream out. When you reach the limit
of the mind's endurance
imagine leaves on a birch outside the room:

the wind dances them
in sunlight, each serrated edge defined
with terrible precision
against the brilliant bark.

2.
Think if you can bear it of Barvenkovo:
your father's hands clamp you hard
into the chair, the tobacco smell
of the doctor's coat, bluestone
burning the underside of your eyelids.
Remember Boris who ran screaming away to hide.
Think of your brother blind.

3.
Coming home
it is the blurred silence
you must prepare for.
The bandages your hands abhor,
the apparent absence of the right side
of vision. Strangers
entering your room, spilling comfort
cold liquid in your eye.

Cut off from the blue climbing clematis
the blinding marigolds ·
you will be a wanderer now turning east
now west. You will return often

to that other country, the precise
shore of childhood. The pale Russian steppe
rolled out like gold under your feet,
the bronze marker on your mother's grave.
Smoke in slender columns floats up
from the village. Both eyes follow
its delicate rising to the sky.

Agenda

Evenings I meet my kin
in rooms overlooking the Assiniboine
River. A coy crescent moon
flickers through elm tree skeletons.
Lights from opposite apartments
shiver on dark water.

The rooms are well-lit and littered
with fragments of white picket fences
the winter flight through Poland
typhoid fever
and a string of stone flour mills
towering over cobbled streets
in Barvenkovo.

We've each brought something.
I a fistful of stories
my mother told me about summer
in Yalta. Hilda offers coffee
unfolds old letters from the dead.

If I listen sharply
past the conversation
I hear the red and white
noise of armies, cries of women
splitting the night, the grinding traffic
below us on Grosvenor Street.

Peter Kornelius Froese
born and buried in a vanished village
somewhere in the Ukraine. We've lost the name
of his first wife. We need evidence
that his twelve sons our grandfathers lived

where we say they lived
completed what we believe.

This is October. We pledge our words
we'll track down each fact
faithfully by April. May at the latest.
Tomorrow we'll rake the last brown leaves
wrap gunny sacks around rose bushes
and brace for winter.

Artist and Medium

A Curious Beatitude
(Upon hearing Brahms's *Ein Deutsches Requiem*)

1. *Selig sind die da Leid tragen*
(Blest are those who carry sorrow)

Now everything is ready. Lights in the concert hall
dim down. Up on stage, the maestro
cues chorus and orchestra. An overture
and the *requiem* begins.

Congolese women lithe as saplings
balance firewood, baskets of mangoes,
manioc soaked in the river
and sorrow on their heads.

No one knows what grief the woman down the street
conceals, lugging laundry to the laundromat,
groceries in clumsy bags to the parked van,
her cranky child from the garage to house to bed.

And Eve. She must have carried sorrow like a stone.
First son a murderer, second murdered,
the seductive apple tree, the garden
gone for good.

Voices and violins carry the melody
with gravity. It floats up to the loges,
balconies lean in. There's an almost-gasp,
a bursting in the ear, a curious

unstopping. In the darkened hall,
lightness, as if a load is jettisoned.
As if an albatross-
burden slides into the sea.

2. *Denn alles Fleisch es ist wie Grass*
(For all flesh is as grass)

Lately I am weight-lifting to curb upper arm flab.
Call it penitence. Call it atonement
for transgression and omission. I am listening
to the CBC's long litany: surfeit of sweetness,
meals cooked up too swiftly.
Our children burdened with obesity.

Hamlet proclaimed flesh *too, too solid.*
Wanted it melted.
A melancholic strain had long hummed in his veins.
He's been pale for centuries and thin, though wiry.
When his body's blood is poisoned, spilt,
before the arm that dropped the rapier stiffens,
before *flights of angels* catch the conductor's cue,

he'll rise, unsteady, on one elbow from his death,
speak with a princely voice, not of time's brevity
but its continuance.

The hall is hushed
in expectation of a reverent entry,
free of weight, into a rest so absolute, so still
you hear breath rise, a vapour from the prairie's lung.
Buffalo grass, foxtail, thin blades of bluestem
singing.

3. *Herr, lehre doch mich*
Das ein Ende mit mir haben muss
(Lord, teach me that my end must come)

A child aces addition and subtraction,
masters multiplication, even long division,
may one day sail through geometry, adore algebra,
trip over trigonometry,
and despite titillating correlation
between music and mathematics,
decline calculus.

A lovely, random ray of light erases
calculations on a flip chart.
Obliterates the glitches on a page.

End of day:
What has the homework-toting, dawdling child
left to get by heart? What lesson
waits in the suburban street, the lane, the concrete
driveway leading home?

(Will the child thrive? Will languages,
philosophy, material sciences, the law
stake claims? Awaken curiosity?
Will he or she love rock, jazz, classical music?
Appreciate the cadence of a *requiem*?)

The child, half-grown, slows down
for cracks in the asphalt,
hesitates at empty corners,
stalls beside an overflowing trash can,
the squashed body of a swallow unaccountably fallen

and stops

as if to calculate. As if
to let an unpredicted
probability
sink in.

4. *Wie lieblich sind deine Wohnungen*
(How lovely are your dwellings)

Almost overnight, an excavation. Walls roughed up,
roof pitched on the vacant property.
Structure displacing emptiness. Construction
crews where casual cats and the wind roamed.

No one's children played there.
No one restrained the dandelions.
Fences sag as if their joints are worn.
Paint peels like desiccated skin.

Your aging father after supper begs:
take me home. He knows wherever home is,
it's not here. Not this third floor cell,
this loneliness, this meagre light.

Where shall we house the weariness?
What dwelling's cosy and commodious,
illuminated but not blinding, workmanship
still under warranty, air uniformly wholesome?

To complete the picture you will need trees
planted near a lucent stream, fruit ripening,
birds light as dandelion down seeking respite
from the never-setting sun. And carolling.

5. *Ihr habt nun Traurigkeit*
(You have sorrow now)

This is by far *The Saddest Music in the World.*
You want it sung when hope is laid to rest
like the fallen vireo a gardener finds and cradles
in earth. You want it for the children
hunkered near graves of mothers
and fathers dead of AIDS in Africa.

You want this music for your swan song
when you leave unwillingly
the stage where you have flickered
briefly, rarely
shone, and sometimes strutted stupidly.

When you are far from home you want
its gloomy harmonies, its downcast beauty.

> The first notes came to Brahms
> when death had put an end to Robert
> Schumann's music. A companionship.
> Brahms wrung from that bereavement
> cadences. When his beloved mother died
> the music kept on coming. Out of grief
> he made a *Requiem*, in German.
> Out of sorrow, solace.

Neither the treble voices of The Anonymous Four
lamenting unaccompanied the plight of wayfaring
strangers yearning for a sweet hereafter,
nor the minor melodies an orthodox male choir sings
evenings, *a capella,* during Lent,
nor blues nor jazz can offer this much
sadness. It leaves you curiously

undone. It leaves you
comforted.

6. *Denn wir haben hie keine bleibende Stadt*
(We have no permanent city here)

Baghdad bombed. New York assaulted
on a flawless, teal-blue morning,
Jerusalem built on rubble of the blest
city once named Salem.

Invisible cities Calvino conjured shimmer
behind closed eyes. Ancient Atlantis,
somnolent under water, waits
for a not-yet-born Ulysses to locate it.

> Woodwinds and grieving strings
> accompany the yearning of soprano, alto,
> tenor and baritone, for the city of peace,
> unmarred, illuminated, permanent.

Will TV kids, afflicted with
unsightly wounds earth-dwellers carry,
believe hope is not lost, not all
have lost it? In New York

architects draft blueprints of a future
habitation in the emptiness. In Baghdad
looters scrabbling through rubble
excavate from under time and twisted steel:

antiquities. Their worth soars way beyond
words. Try saying them. Say: *Tigris*
and Euphrates. Say: *Eden*. Say: *garden*.
The tree of life. The golden apple.

Slowly, with what's left of breath, say
Salem.

7. *Selig sind die Toten*
(Blest are the dead)

A blessing before those most needing it leave.
The anthem fades. The last clump of earth
thuds on the coffin lid. The undertaker offers
the bereaved blood-red carnations
shrouded in a brace of baby's breath.

Mourners rally around last words,
last wishes. They must negotiate life
insurance, unpaid debts,
testaments, unlisted
objects waiting for possession.

Those left behind could use a blessing.
Memory of derailed or broken off
conversations erased. Rift and rending
assuaged. A retroactive
reconciliation.

But this beatitude's intended for the dead
as though, although departed, they remain
with us. As if sorrow becomes blessing;
poverty an asset; loss, gain. As if
the earth that covers them still
waits to be inherited.

Artist and medium

Martyrdom like radiance of a clear night sky
can leave you baffled. Jan Luyken finds no words for it
although he's written love lyrics, painted
morning and evening in pale tones. He knows

delicate brush strokes can't take hold of this
triumphant dying: a song torn from between charred lips
the way a sword's torn from the heart.
Jan chooses a needle and begins

dribbling acid on a copper plate. He's pleased
with the austerity of etching the fine line
between agony and exultation,
between silence and breath. He tries defining

faith: should it be modest or bold,
reasonable, fervent, fanatical? He's drawn to the plain
homeliness of bound hands
and feet, a stretched wrist, bones stripped clean

the raw texture of freshly seared skin. He's engraved
the afternoon mob taunting the condemned
for heresy, the executioner
for a job badly done.

He's mastered the way the greedy flames reach out
for flesh, a child's hand
for its doomed mother, the impatient soul
ecstatically for God.

Jan Luyken
1649–1712

Guide to the KGB Museum
(Vilnius, 2001)

The courthouse door slams shut behind you
like a gunshot. A sentence against light.
Stone steps descend to the cells' dark territory,
a clammy underworld. A bitter country
that you, free traveller, not guiltless, but not yet condemned,
selected from museums listed in the latest
Vilnius in Your Pocket.

Prisoners with empty pockets slept
empty of hope
on unrelenting beds, walls dripping
moisture like bleached blood.

Ice water fills the concrete basin in the torture cell.
Spent from interrogation, taunts, repeated beatings,
lack of sleep, the depleted body,
well-worn punching bag,
with one dull splash
falls in.

A guardroom is a prison too: guards forced
to restrain, deprive, grind down
the breathing dead, who hold
eternity in pulsing hearts.

A narrow corridor, a row of peepholes
straight from a Solzhenitsyn novel. Trapdoors
to squeeze tin bowls of watery gruel through.
Soup with fish heads.
Dry bread. The heartsick, hollow prisoner will take
and eat.

For the inmate gone berserk with memory:
gestures, touch of living loved ones, glances,
doubts of innocence,
the walls in this next cell are padded.
Solitude without solace.

The doomed lie sleepless
on the eve of execution. Bleak rooms
crammed with emptiness. No space
for tables, chairs, false hope
of deliverance. No room
for light.

En route to death, the condemned
cross (shackled) a fenced-in yard:
scant metres of earth, the rationed sky, a quick
snatch of air that holds the agonized
sweet scent of home.

Now slip these grey shrouds over your shoes.
You will walk on sacred ground. On grief. On glass
through which a bed of sand is visible. Bones
buried like history in dust. Scraps of cloth,
leather that might have been a belt.

Pockmarks in the concrete wall:
bullets that flesh and bone could not resist
set like jewels in cement.
All hope (abandoned in a structure built
for justice) stopped here.

Blood has been washed away
but the stench endures. It mingles with the sweet
perfume of lilacs, lilies of the valley, yellow roses
hawked in the cobbled city streets.

It clings to your skin. You can smell it
in the chestnut trees that every spring
lift candles to the sky.

What the boat carries

On the churning sea a small blue boat.
Wind smooths the yellow sail and pins it flat
against the fitful sky. Sky over Galilee
was agitated, water olive-
green, white-capped and snarling.

Two shrouded figures in the stern. Women?
Which one's the sailor, which one prophesies
rough passage? Four able hands lie idle.
The travellers look ahead, steadfast, as if
they've seen Christ walking on the waves.

Who are they?
Why did they embark?
What voice or circumstance persuaded them
to climb in-
to the empty hold?

They've brought no luggage for the voyage.
No munchies, no bottle of water.
No oars and no one asleep in the hold.
There's no visible tiller. Not one life preserver.
What absent captain guides this boat,

the yellow sail so radiant it blinds?
Pigment laid on with zeal. The artist's
vision of arrival at safe harbour,
desire to awaken sleepers,
to catch before storm breaks

above the hollow boat a blazing
portion of the sun.

Odilon Redon (1840–1916)
Mystical Boat, pastel and black chalk on buff-coloured wove paper

Fiction

The room is occupied, the queen-sized bed
made up, immaculate. So ordinary,
chocolates and a pink rose on the pillow
would be absurd.

Closed luggage in a corner on the floor.
A ridiculous hat struts on the shelf and a floral
dress lies draped, defeated on the green chair.
Fiction lurks in the freshly painted corners.

Like sleuths pursuing source and efficacy
of light, we scan the hotel room walls:
a large pale panel and the smaller square, opaque,
egg-yellow. Egg shell draperies pass muster.

And now we can no longer disregard
the woman sitting on the bed, half-nude,
her brooding face, her still-young body shadowed,
a folded letter in her birdlike hands.

It's not her semi-nakedness alone disturbs
nor ink-black shadows under the bed.
Not knowing which bright panel is the window
troubles us.

Not knowing the letter's intent. The sender.
A single sentence could condemn the woman:
she'd be obliged to throw her dress on, don the hat,
grab the unopened bags. She'd thrust her feet into

the kicked-off, high-heeled shoes we overlooked,
and leaving no excuses for the viewer, no note, no tip

at the front desk, check out of the newly-painted room.
The meticulous hotel.

Edward Hopper (1882–1967)
Hotel Room, 1931, oil on canvas

Letters from Siberia

(Based on drawings and texts
by Jakob Sudermann, 1888–1940)

1.
Dear Gretel I am sending you
a butterfly a bee bunches of daisies
and a cat I had intended to send
a mouse also but it got away
not all mice are so quick
or so lucky

There are no butterflies here
no bees no daisies
it is winter and the ice thick
paper your mother sent
is gone the colours finished
when next I stumble upon
blank scraps the fortuitous
small stub of a pencil

I will draw the garden blooming
in my head and if they let me
I will send it I will leave it
to your mother to describe
fountains at Alexeyevka
carriage and matched horses
rose beds how the sun
warmed our world

she will tell you
I am the lost Onkel
whom you do not know
the one who sketched

a family dwelling painted
the orchard in autumn painted
your grandmother at prayer
or sewing painted the snow
that fell on the Dnieper River
and one day in spring
vanished

2.
Dear Gretel I can see my breath
all afternoon in the endless evening
stars are my candle how long
before a pinpoint of cold light
reaches me and keeps me
hoping the longed-for warmth is
somewhere on its way

don't be afraid if this should be
my last letter if the picture
of the garden I remember
never reaches you
the sun will rise rain fall
on Alexeyevka I believe
you will see spring

3.
Dear Gretel it is spring
your Onkel who is still as much
alive as the mangy cat
though aged imagines
himself in Alexeyevka
he is too weak to mount
the black stallion
climb the greening hills
too weak to imagine painting

the budding apricot trees
even the sun rising
earlier each day
can not warm him
after the long and bitter winter
a small grey mouse appeared
and this time it did not
escape

A Matter of Language

Language arts

From my side of the desk
I dispense connectives
guaranteed to link thoughts
and speech smooth as honey
phrases graced with simile
resonant vowels
verbs reverberating
confident as trumpets
their message unmistakable

When the bell rings
they scatter   disconnected
fragments
dangling dangerously
free
from sense or structure

The metaphors they grasp
have motors revved for violent rhetoric
they choose raw decibels
unmodified beat that speaks
persuasively to fluent limbs
eyes electric with understanding
superlative and running on
beyond the need for words

Mine echo in the empty room
and settle harmlessly
into the chalk dust

Evidence

Evenings I read the journals my students keep
because I tell them to. They confess everything
I've always suspected. Concealed hatred of the dark
a crippling residue of childhood
nothing can root out. Terror of mad dogs, death
unguarded heights. A few are desperate enough
to admit the unspeakable dread
of failure.

When I've read everything I asked for, all
the terrible softness their tough nouns and verbs
can't hide, the undeniable evidence of breaking
at the edges, there is nothing
I can do. Nothing
except point out perhaps the lack
of punctuation, circle the misspelled words
with a soft pencil, join
all disconnected fragments. From now on

sleeping or waking I carry this dead weight
of evidence everywhere, implicated
by its terrible clarity. Stripped
by my own witness
of innocence and every alibi.

Remembering

Poppies I've offered them
this morning row by row
are strewn on the grey tiled floors
in corridors and classrooms
like random splashes of spilt blood.

They slip unhindered
from pastel trenches of shaker-knit sweaters
from t-shirts and stubborn textures of acid-
washed jean jackets.
Black leather rejects them outright.

One boy picks them up from the dust
where they've fallen
one by one, trampled under legions of Reeboks.
He sticks them on his Roots shirt
and wears them, a chestful of medals,
all afternoon.

Some have remembered
quarters and dimes
a few loonies for the white box.

Remembrance I tell them
is what we offer the dead.
My students are only remotely familiar
with death. Pepsis and popcorn
guard them against shattering
machinegunfire, screams of the lost, bombs
exploding and other sound effects.

I've been spared too.
My fathers and grandfathers

all pacifists
tell me no bloody stories of Normandy
or Dieppe. The death they warn me of
is everlasting. There's no hope
of glory and all remembering
will be sheer hell.

A matter of language

Your being here
(and mine)
has everything to do
with language:
your inability to speak
(clearly enough by my standards)
hope and desire; mine
(by yours)
to articulate affliction.

In the classroom
on opposite sides
of the desk
we heard about the violent
border incident.

Language
or lack of it
can not protect flesh
against the brute thrust
of bayonets,
cold malice of bullets.

You knew this,
mutely. I
on the other hand
wanted words
to complete the suffering.
Flesh out, so to speak,
utter
this deadly, this
unspeakable assault.

And the music

A mute circle of flattened grass
blades bent or broken
dark stains the uniformed arm
points out. The murdered girl
smiles on the evening news, her eyes
her fine black hair, mouth
made static and so brief.

The rest of the evidence
pulses in my skull like the untamed beat of drums,
the mournful strumming of a single guitar
in moonlight. Concealed
in dissonant shadows of cottonwood
hard fingers of men not yet grown old
play savage melodies on a delicate string.
Cut short her throat's wild throbbing.

Silence
clamps the quivering body, a cold
iron stranglehold. Bones crush
easily as love. No sign of struggle.
No screams.

A sudden dull knowing
descends like the hard blow of a blunt instrument.
They say the festival music faded
somewhere before daybreak.

On the last day of school
a student tells me she'll camp weekends
at Bird's Hill Park or near
the pine-edged lake her family loves. She'll dance
all night on the beach. Laughter of friends

mingles with night wind
and the music
from radios. Waking she finds herself
on sand warmed by the sun.

Because she is young, her limbs
a shimmering cadence, hair, skin lyrical,
my throat goes dry. I cannot say *Be careful.*
There are dark forests in the heart. Stay close
to the light of the sun
and fire. Close to the music.

I want to be deaf
to the violent dirge of lake waves.
The hard wild song of blood on a summer night.

Advent: Montreal, 1989

We light the first candle for Advent:
waiting that ends always in death
more brutal than expected. (Birth
first, a sharp gleam of joy.
A small cry leaps out:

My God!)

The flame throws light and shadow
on dead faces of fourteen young
women, their skin grey, shrunk
under the sudden knowledge of all
malice, all bitterness.
The stiffening hands empty. Fear
widens the eyes.

How silently
flesh opens to receive
bullets, bayonets, nails.

We strike more matches with hands
cold as stone, clutch uneasy candles
in each hard fist.

A radio in the abandoned cafeteria
serves carols to the shocked walls.

In the violated classroom
chalk dust settles quietly
into the twilight.
Like snow.

Window

Something in the classroom has shifted
while your back was turned. Those tall, clever
boys in dark jackets have invented
a brand new game. They do not need you
to explain its aim, rules, etiquette.
While you were listing on the chalkboard
texts to be read, projects due, attitudes
to overhaul, language to shape up
or ban from future use,
the girls left their desks. They are waiting
in line at the window, their summery dresses
radiant in sunlight, their silken haloes
teased by a southerly breeze. While you
add to a list the names of those guilty
of insubordination, tardiness, opinions,
the last pretty girl slips through the open window.
You are just in time to catch a glimpse of one
white ankle sock.

Colours at the Border

Warning

You'll find bodies abandoned at the border:
a random scattering of shadows
on one side or another of made barriers, strung
barbed across the everyday

landscape. These faces, arms, legs that moved
once, were animated
mark now the boundary between silence and breath,
order and reprehensible disorder.

Wire-thin lines divide us
the way the horizon divides darkness from day.
Uneasy travellers mark fear at every border:
hands fashioned for warm comfort become fists,

iron-hard. Fingers reach for the trigger,
or else hang slack, emptied of all desire
before they stiffen. The eyes,
desperate for another country,

for the last frail light, remain wide
open and so terrified.

Colours at the border

Absence of colour at the border
is not neutrality. Nor is it merely dull
camouflage. This blandness
is denial: a uniform state of mind.
Stubborn reluctance ever to say yes
to radiance, the sky's blue reach,
a reed flute's fragile melody
free-floating in a windowed room.

A kind of terror, knowing
the wind blows where it will.

On the way to the border we passed
poppies, blood-red, their petals
radiant. Stems bending
freely to the wind in the unrestrained
widening of green fields.

Seven-year-old girl in a studio

She is contained. Not in the softly-powered pastel
dress, her tattered little sandals, sun-bleached hair.
I think of poppies I saw dancing in a field
contained in brilliance in the gusty wind. But there's no wind
around this girl, no blazing colour, no circumference.
Yet she's contained:

takes paper from a shelf, takes paint, selects a brush
and finds a quiet sun-lit place. Pours water from a jar.
Each brush stroke is a solemn item in a creed
she's unaware of. Where does the vision come from
that becomes a garden
shining as if it's washed by recent rain

the morning sun makes diamonds of? A yellow bird
hovers and broods as if in benediction over leaves and over
each wet flower pressing purple
and pink and saffron to the paper's edge
spilling its buoyant colour like spontaneous prayer
past boundaries and over

everything. She gathers with a gentle confidence
with tiny hands the paper, paint, the entire
garden, carries it to a shelf as if it's nothing and yet
something that she loves. She moves
empty-handed through the door and past
the limits of my vision

leaving the table bare, the whole room filled
with scent of flowers, traces of
her movements, stir of wind.
I am surrounded by the invisible
flight of birds. The silent breathing
of unhindered presence.

Health measures

1.
Bring your children to the sea. Bury them chin deep
in warm sand, watch their bones grow straight and firm.
Believe me their blue eyes will turn brilliant as the summer
sky. No fragment of amber on the wide beach too small or
insignificant in their strong fingers.

2.
Promise me you'll wear this crude bit of amber always
around your neck, next to the skin and I'll promise you
long life for your body. Healing for your heart.

This is not magic, although it is a secret kept in trees
and in the sea. In the sun's endless rising and setting
matter may turn translucent. More beautiful than gold.

3.
I'll remember you running ahead of me, headlong
into the sea, the sun igniting your pale hair, turning
your uplifted hands to fire. You expected me to follow.

It's not as if I refused to recognize my need
for healing. But you were always ahead of me,
your perfect body buoyant, joy-filled. I imagined

your muscles, blood vital. I envied you,
believed you steadfast as the women in your legends.
And all sea water ice-cold.

4.
Plant a garden, grow berries for winter.
White, red and black currants, for instance. Colours

you believe should leave no room for doubt. White stands
variously for purity of heart and innocence or complete
failure of courage, ill health. Take your pick. Black
requires no explanation and as for red you may see it as
a stain on the earth or marking, darkly, the doorposts.

5.
Rub ruta for whole minutes into the skin of your fingertips.
Then lift them like this. The heavy scent of innocence and
freedom stings your nostrils. Let it. And do not mistake the
dizziness for victory. It's not that simple.

6.
In the sanctity of this oak forest, renew your vows.
Resolve to be resolute, push deeper into the barbed
underbrush you fear for its shadows. The absence of light
leaves you trembling. The noise is always more than the wind,
or footfalls on dry leaves, or birdwings or your obstinate
heart beating. More than foreign voices clashing mid-air.

Learn your fears by heart and then confess them, here
on the forest's moss-floor. Believe me only then
these gnarled branches, emerald leaves, the rough-ridged
trunks of oak become a sanctuary. A place where you may heal.
Or if need be, hide.

Triptych

1.
Old women at the market weigh mountains
of huge gooseberries, cucumber pyramids, plums
on an ancient scale. They exchange dried herbs

for roubles. The roses you desire
must be white. Unopened. *In odd numbers,*
they warn you, *to escape death.* Walk circumspectly

home across the sombre square, evading cracks
in the pavement. These green thorns
press delicate lacerations into your warm hand.

2.
Sun plunges orange, flaming
down the blue-grey, anonymous sky.
The scarred TV tower a dark sword's thrust

above the crosses. Candles flicker
a silent mourning. Press your face to the fence.
Look, you can see armed guards

beside the tower. Tanks.
Everything this side of the horizon bound,
shackled in black wreaths of rusted razorwire.

3.
In this country you find Christ
carved from hard-grained oak. He waits
mournfully at the foot of a hill

beside stone walls or at a roadside
grown familiar. His affliction
travels with you. His chiselled body

bowed. His barbed head rests
on peasant fingers that grip the wood
weathered and grey as grief.

What we want

Where have they gone? The quiet
bodies decomposing, burnt to ash,
scattered. Wherever
they are, they continue to exist
in photo albums, home videos,
in our hearts. We imagine them

arriving at some shore
no eye has ever seen
and no ear heard the haunting
language of its music. A country
no one's mapped, no one's travelled
and returned from.

We want them back. Or else
somewhere at rest and without fear
of AIDS, the West Nile virus, SARS.
We want them where they have no need
for respirators, wheelchairs, frequent MRIs,
puffers, pills for under the tongue,

no need to carry with them where they go
the weight of pain. Dull grudges. Guns.
Or guilt.
We want them where one day,
alive
and unencumbered,
we will find them.

Beauty

1.

Rats rustling in the dark, odours of death in every corner.
But you, Etty, on your hard bunk, are still among the living.
Beyond the barracks, beyond barbed wire, you imagine
a field of lupine. An easy leap from that to jasmine
blooming beside a window in Amsterdam
where you rode your bicycle beside the canal,
boarded any tram you pleased, strolled evenings
with your lover past the skating club.

If you cannot sleep it is not sheep you count
but next day's duties. Soup for the mother of a newborn.
Rusks for N who cannot eat hot food. Another letter
to be written (filched paper, borrowed pencil)
to an address in Amsterdam, begging for a coat,
a loaf of bread. Words to a world that will forget,
but is not forgotten in Westerbork. In the morning,
lupine blooming yellow on the heath, you will rise,

take the hand of a terrified child, keep vigil
with an old man's fear of death. Barbed wire is real;
hatred futile. You refuse to the end to give up the anguish
of remembering, feeling, thinking: Dostoyevsky,
Rilke, and the dear man (no longer with the living)
who spoke to you of love, read from the gospels
words that keep you as you keep them in your heart
underneath the yellow star where you store all
the beauty you see everywhere in Westerbork.

2.

The train is waiting. You have packed
your little Bible, diaries, the Russian grammar book,
and Tolstoy. This time
it is your name on the list and you must go

east in a baggage car. The overloaded
train will leave; you will arrive
at a destination you refuse to dread,
a place from where no traveller returns.

Will you dare tell those
whose terror and despair crowd the train
that you have looked and always found
life filled with meaning?

Afterwards it will be said:
She left Westerbork
singing.

Still Life with Light

Prairieology

Prairie's the preferred home of the gopher.
It slips into an earthen orifice
pops up again, alert
curious
and startled by the merest whiff of danger
once more disappears.

Prairie winds
unhindered
abscond with topsoil
hasten tumbleweed along.

Framed by the oceanic sky
meadowlarks warble: matins, vespers, laud.
Red-winged blackbirds perch, wind-tousled
sentinels on weathered fence posts.

Clouds drift, round-bellied
fantasies across the firmament.
Horizon's elusive thread goes on and on
receding.

Time stands still.

> *O God of prairie grasses*
> *tumbleweed*
> *bleached bison bones*
> *monarch of butterflies*
> *birds gophers the unbridled*
> *wind*
>
> *here I stand*
> *roofless*

miniscule in this flat vastness
terrified of storm
crack of thunder
lightning's fire-fork.
I am listening
for the wind to lose its bluster
stop howling from the west
breathe gently
whisper through me. Until then
O sovereign of hiding places
shelter me

Tree

I dreamt a tree, neither pine nor palm,
in a country I had never travelled.
Storms that decimated poplar, birch, and willow
could not disturb its sturdy canopy.
Its fruit ripened where the hungry gathered,
where refugees and strangers rested. I dreamt
a slither in the grass beside a river
that flows through a garden. When I awoke,
the tree woke with me. Its leaves
shone green in vacant spaces of the day,
at the crossroads of simplicity and fear,
lethargy and reconciliation,
alpha and omega.

Matins II

Morning and I'm pouring milk in my coffee
spreading marmalade on bread.
Sun floods in
dodging the ash tree's branches, invoking
the colour of irises in a faded tablecloth.
Apples in the bowl glow, everything haloed
in radiance. I should be glad for
this outpouring of warmth and light
hold it in my brain, bathe in it.
And I *would* except for the fettering
knowledge of the perfect day lily's
fading. The implacable transience
of hummingbirds.

After a long winter

Back yard and garden inundated.
Trunk of the leafless ash tree,
the squirrel running rag-tailed along
the wire fence, town houses turned upside down
in icy water. At night stars and the moon
mirrored in a frozen lake.
So much snow this winter
we were afraid it would never melt.
We abandoned hope

like those forlorn disciples, bereft of light,
tasting the bitter slowness of that sombre Sabbath,
afraid it would never end. Death
victorious after all: God buried.
The doomed sun pulled like a prisoner down
and down to the grim horizon. The unconsolable wind
breathing unspeakable grief. At the city's edge
the empty outstretched arms of three
abandoned crosses.

Still life with light

Peeling an orange this morning
    and planning lunch (a quiche
    green salad, croissant)
thinking there's nothing lovely
as light on still life
    a bowl of fruit, a green wine bottle
    white rumpled tablecloth, pure
    morning turning the muted background
    bright.

Sun pouring on field lilies
on sparrows that fly or fall
spills on my table radiant as rain,
blinds, warms before it shifts
shimmering from the east window.

I reach for another wedge
of orange
suck juice from my fingers.
The light's there too
and will be

on five or six of us gathered
at my table. Every move we make,
the quick tilting of a head,
lift of a hand, each glance
invites light. Dark things
we'll speak from the heart or leave
unspoken as we eat (salad
            croissant, quiche)
will be there too
the shadows growing

slowly. We'll sip our coffee
until someone rises, remembering
amazed, the dentist, hair dresser, post
office, the shopping mall,
leaving a cup half   full, the rest of us
choosing fruit from the glass bowl,
brushing crumbs from the rumpled tablecloth
or just sitting
still.

Two crows

I heard twa corbies making a mane—ANONYMOUS

A pair of crows perched like closed books on the wire fence.
They are reading me. Leaving me uneasy. All morning
they flapped up and down, distraught
parents, feeding their wide-mouthed fledglings
nested in the elm whose juicy leaves feed cankerworms.

I'm on the deck munching a tuna sandwich. I've clapped away
grackles, dull-witted rabbits from my lettuce.
Whatever grows lures gluttony. Whatever lives is ravenous.
Legions of forest tent caterpillars, fat slugs, aphids
in the hollyhocks. Across the dust-choked lane,

my neighbour, paper-thin from breast cancer,
brings her book to the window. After a winter of surgery
and chemo, volumes of radiation, light swims through her.
Only a miracle, she says, will shrink the canker in her chest,
and deep sleep silence the brash crows, blot out
the hungry shadow of their wings.

gospel

a ruffled sparrow flung splat against the glass
a brown blossoming, a residue
pasted on sheer light

I'm in the east window reading the gospel (not
where God sees the sparrow fall
counts every hair)

maybe I'll see the smashed bird
returned to earth in spring under the juniper
unless the grey cat gets there first

(*what do you want me to do for you* he says
to the blind man as though it's not obvious
the weight of walking alone scared in the dark

street leaves you speechless
paralyzed as well as blind) it's possible
the sparrow's only stunned

will lift its wings (a miracle)
and fly warbling its way to the nest
the roof, the sky

me still reading at the window and the cat
purring, licking her gleaming fur
while everything under the sun
turns quietly to fire

Alpha and Omega

In the garden

Then God said, Let us make humankind in our image—GENESIS 1.26

What were you thinking, God? In spring
the boulevards strut their tenderest green
spun in your brain. Tantalizing birdsong,
fragrances float straight to the head. The heart,
as you well know, falters.
We'll regularly fail to tend the garden,
forget to feed the animals. Apples
will be wasted. How extravagantly

beautiful the blossoms are on shrubs and trees
in May. Impatient, we want fruit, not green,
but glowing. Want to sink our teeth
into the flesh of apricots. Our tongues crave
taste of apples.

What were you thinking, leaving us in charge,
giving us dominion, as if we were fit
to be emperors, chief executives, micro or macro
managers, as if we understood
words like *tend, wait patiently* and *multiply?*

As if we were able with our wayward minds
to imagine mercy's breadth and wideness,
had ears to hear, could learn to linger
long enough to taste and see.

patriarchs

have you heard
about Abraham, the old man
asks   (he's got asthma
his chest heaves
and falls
and heaves)

Abraham had faith, he gasps
followed God half-
way around the world
lived in tents
got rich

entertained angels
in the great shade of an oak

the small boy backs away
wide-eyed   afraid
from that day
Abraham has thin white hair
a bent back and
gasps for air

Hagar

Foreigner. Female. Slave.
With such a resumé, what chance has she got

even though she can kill a lamb, cook it,
sweep the floor of the master's tent.

Youth and fertility are both
good news and bad. When all is said and done,

we find her hiding in the desert,
the sun a fireball.

She's not the first woman to find herself
pregnant, alone, facing the essential questions:

Where are you from
and where do you think you're going?

Hot, heavy, afraid,
she faces the Hebrew God, desperate

to know what lies at the heart of this deity
she cannot see. The blazing desert sun

beats down and plain truth dawns:
You are the One who sees me.

The child stirs in her belly.

Pharaoh's daughter

I pull you crying from reeds, raise you
in the shade of palm-fringed pyramids
in the midst of chanting priests
and alabaster.

Who would have dreamed
you'd choose to champion
a pack of quarrelsome brickmakers.

You abandon the sacred
river, trail a lonely god
who gives you burning bushes
endless wasteland.

You tear my heart.

I gave you gold
enough, and slaves.
Enduring promises of Egypt.

In the potter's house

So I went down to the potter's house,
and I saw him working at the wheel.—JEREMIAH 18.3

It's not the monotonous dull
whirring of the wheel
shards scattered all over
the earthen floor
or even the dank half-darkness
catch the imagination
of the prophet.

He doesn't mind the wet smell
filling his lungs
the taste of clay on his lips.

The potter's moist palms
shape the unhardened clay
pressing it out
of its heavy earth-brown
formlessness
urging escape
from the wheel's hypnotic song.

The prophet is amazed
to see the loveliness
the potter keeps hidden
deep in his fingers
or somewhere in his heart or brain
break free and spill

over in bowls vases cups
each curve perfect
each premeditated lip and throat

graceful. The potter
while the prophet watches
slides them with shard-
lacerated hands
into the white flame.

The potter

So I went down to the potter's house,
and I saw [her] working at the wheel.—JEREMIAH 18.3

Coming in from the wind, dishevelled, we cluster
like commas around the woman at the wheel.
Her foot moves up and down. Hands cup the clay,
centring, altering, coaxing it upward. We grow alert
as exclamation points. The matter in the potter's hand
gains shape: a bowl, lip like a wing, round belly.
Her fingers cradle the emerging form, emending it
to match the brain's vision. The alluring

object, as we watch, collapses in the brackets
of her hands. With one swift move she scoops it up,
squashes it, a mundane blob of clay.
She doesn't say: That's it. Period.
To question marks surrounding her, she says
she'll rescue that smashed lump tomorrow,
rises, unties the denim apron stained with a residue
of clay, rinses her hands,

waves us to the table.
Coffee is poured into mugs she has made.
Oatmeal raisin cookies, lemon drops. We eat
and leave a scattering of crumbs to punctuate
the lucent pearl-blue glaze of perfect plates
that only yesterday our gracious potter
pulled with her stained, shard-lacerated hands
from the fire.

On the banks of the Nile

So they entered Egypt . . . —JEREMIAH 43.7

All things begin and end
with words. The ones you hear now
jangle like chains. They are foreign
and get distorted in the desert's
blinding sand-storms.

The ones you speak are heavy
as stone. They won't ring out
or echo back from the slant sides
of pyramids.

It wasn't your idea
all those threats and warnings.

Fed up with lamentations
the fugitives from Judah
imagine they could live on bread
and fresh memories of the moon
blessing the beautiful city.

They don't believe you
when you speak of wolves
wild in wheat fields, foxes
skulking in the vineyards.

Last night you dreamt a mother
was eating her new-born child.

Something you learn
living this close to that aching
hunger and death:

there's only so much you can do
with words.

Incarnation

Ezekiel wades knee-deep
through bleached bones.
Marrowless femurs touch shoulder blades
casually, ankle bones
gleaming in the early sun
lean gently against fine hip bones
belonging once to children.

The hills echo the crisp clicking
and clacking around his shins.

It's the smooth gaping skulls
he steers clear of, grimacing
reminders of mortality.

Ezekiel knows no singing
or whistling will make these bones grow
flesh and blood, rise up from the valley floor
leaping and dancing.
Only his walking through them
causes stir. That and the small silk wind
rippling from hills and the sun
sending a shaft of warm light
into the large and small hollows.

Hosea

Clear from the start
she doesn't love you.
She has eyes only for the finest
linen and red wine.
Gold if you can get it for her.
Other men.

She gives you nothing
not even your own children.

You will tear the silver
from her silk neck, the soft white
wool from her back. Plant thorn hedges
across the shady paths she loves
and leave her
naked in forsaken fields.

You'll never take her back
into your arms again
and again with gifts of new grain
and apples, your aching fingers
tender on her lips, your flesh willing
to be broken. Your bewildered heart
listening for her to sing your name.

Zephania

I can't believe the preacher
would choose this sun-bright perfect June
day for a sermon on judgement. Geraniums
strut scarlet along white fences, emerald leaves
glitter with dew. Under blue skies
our polished cars gleam in the street.

We are at peace. We exchange bright words
between prayers, approve the organ prelude
the yellow roses. I browse through
the morning bulletin. Only three chapters

in the prophet Zephania. Skimming images
of closed fists and fire
blood poured out like dust
loud wails from the fishgate, I grope
in growing panic for words
of mercy. There must be grace here
somewhere, before twelve o'clock.
Before the last anthem signals time
for the benediction.

Haggai

There is no poetry in Haggai.
Heaving stones, pounding them
into place, under cleaving heat
of the sun, climbing the steep slopes
to the cedars, hewing pillars
for our God.

We dream
coolness of panelled houses
dream of Babylon. We who have known
rivers more beautiful, swifter
than Jordan. We have forgotten
that former glory, bronze pomegranates
cedar altars overlaid with gold
and gold-faced angels, olive wings
outstretched.

We grow old.
When we drag home sweating
and dust-stained, the prophet
offers promises in prose.

Horizon

It isn't easy writing a poem
about Jesus. You could write the sun
hung low over olive groves
an ancient well in a quaint village
even angels into the landscape.
And blood. But his hard words
his terrible naked mercy
hang like an awkwardness
across a gaunt horizon. His name won't fit
the line's rhythm
unless you make it an expletive
or shape it like a sweet
innocuous philosophy.

It is possible
a poem would lay bare his face
his torn hands
invoke his voice   a hammer
or a bell shattering the crystal morning
at the water's edge
speaking your name and asking
do you love me.

Magnificat

Snow has fallen overnight on roofs of suburban bungalows,
on stiff spirea hedges, on rows of overflowing garbage bins.
Blackbirds occupy a snow-lined poplar branch. Magnificent
in winter white are five wolves cast in bronze
and set in fierce pursuit beside the freeway.
In Bethlehem
there is no snow. Pilgrims armed with bucket lists
crowd the place where twenty centuries ago
they believe a boy was born. The amazed girl-mother
nestled him in straw: a child as perfect as a snowflake.
Mary never knew
the crunch of snow beneath her feet. Sleet
needling her face.
What she was given to know
poured from her mouth like praise. The destitute,
she dared to say, will not always hunger and thirst,
nor will the meek be scattered.
What's high will be brought low.
She might as well have said
bronze wolves will be set free,
spirea hedges shout loud Hallelujahs,
and snow-capped lids of garbage bins
clap noisily for joy.

The night sky

Same old strangers (possibly astrologers,
possibly three) camel their usual way
from east to west crossing blank desert,
time zones. What they are heading for

remains unclear. Under the stingy sun
they trespass foreign fields, prod their animals
past lethargy. How quietly
the winter shadows lengthen,

landscapes shift as if creation, roused,
hopes for release. At nightfall they collapse
beside a meager waterhole. The (possibly hungry,
homesick) travellers before they close their eyes

look up. There is the moon, a flat white stone
embedded in ebony. The faithful constellations.
And just ahead that singular, unerring
blur of light to steer by.

Pileated woodpecker

Sunday morning. Our children shout Hosannas,
wave exuberant palm fronds at the altar,
down the aisle. They follow Jesus—
astride a donkey—through Jerusalem, joyous
procession that within the week draws blood.
The rest of us like stone choose silence.

At the trail head parking lot an afternoon
of chittering sparrows, mud-caked SUVs.
We are waxing skis while halfway up a broken oak
a bird, its broad back facing the people
hacks with no-nonsense purpose at the rough-
ridged bark where its vigorous claws find purchase.

The massive, crimson-crested bird
has come so close, almost among us.
Mesmerized we ogle its body,
admire its plumage, the whole
fierce enterprise. Most of us don't recognize
the amazing creature clamped to its wounded tree.

All afternoon we lean into our chosen trail,
follow its winding way into the woods,
gain speed, gain distance from the dying
echo of that patient hammering.

today

i will live quite simply
as if the hand's clenched fingers
could be persuaded to let go
open like petals of a rose

as if this treacherous lake could bear me
on its rough skin
water come tumbling from a rock
demons from a troubled woman

as if there's a fair chance
coin-stacked tables could be over-turned
the caged bedraggled dove released
the lethal wind beguiled by evening
and by god the dead raised

The race

To the one who conquers . . . —REVELATION 3.21

You are at the beach, reading. Increasing winds
riffle the lake's grey page, puff out slack sails
at the regatta starting line. The windsurfer's wet
suit gleams and the plastic sail he grasps crackles.
Clouds take the shape of an Olympic swimmer
seen in the pool from below, executing the crawl,
arms reaching out like overeager wings. A whistle
signals the start of the race. Let's say the open

book is a Bible. A breeze flips the pages,
Genesis to Revelation, a narrative that holds
within it both the sailor and the sail. Are you
surprised it ends in metaphor? Not a cup
but a crown. Your new name plainly carved
in white stone. The promised morning star.

Alpha and Omega

Let there be light! A flash, a bolt, a brilliant blaze
that puts the kibosh on chaos. Let light shine on width, breadth,
depth, a dazzle to illuminate all matter everywhere. Let it glint
gloriously off ocean wave, sea swell, a brooklet's little ripples.

Let fish rejoice in it fantastically, the fur of fox, cat, cougar,
coyote be haloed. Let light's hot pulse pull prairie grass and
milkweed up to verdant growth, turn grain from green to gold.
In every garden everywhere let peonies, preposterous

begonias unfold. Let every butterfly, bat, bird bathe in radiance.
Let light pour mornings into breakfast bowls, fill empty cups
to overflowing. At evening, let light's mauve plumes linger
on every atom of creation. When darkness closes in,

shrouding the valley floor,
let sky be spangled still, lit with the glow of meteors,
the murky Milky Way, the white-hot stars. O Light of life,
Light of the wobbling world: your splendour does not tarnish,

will not be overcome by random avalanche,
smart missile, guns, flood, smoke of forest fire.
You melt the iron grip of fear. The stone-cold,
guarded grave can never hold you.

Simone Weil: *Pensées*

Beginning

In the beginning the world bursts open
a shimmering opal. In the Luxembourg Gardens
birds carol, an iridescent twittering of joy.
The dew-wet morning grass moves like the sea.

Nights those reticent pin-point stars appear
neither cold nor distant. (What do I know
of distance?)
                                        I touch them

with my new-born fingertips, trace the diamond
rhythm of their music. Proof enough
(I am sure these fervent days) of truth.
I have no need for words that promise love. No need

for further evidence. The madly spinning
and expanding universe
holds for one fragile moment
only light.

Hunger I

I was born hungry.
Nothing in the whole world would ever be enough.
Daybreak to dusk my small mouth gaping
like a bird's for food.
It wasn't mother-milk, her warm breasts given
gladly, my father's need to make things better
I desired.

Only blue sky, the stunning depth of it,
a sudden harmony of curved light, an organ chord
could prune the sharpest edge off
my wanting. How should they have known,
my mother, my kind father:
their joined flesh, satisfied,
could generate voraciousness,
spawn such unseemly thirst and this
unearthly appetite.

Adolescence

I did not care to inhabit entirely my childlike body which I despised for its frailty and complete absence of grace. *Why don't you comb your hair* they said. *Pay more attention to the style and colour of your clothes.* But I lived mainly in my head where I was most at home. Where I considered in the brain's free convolutions the brute force of necessity, learned the torment of attending to an absolute truth not yet defined although its thin edge grew and grew until it tore cruelly at my heart.

About this time the headaches started, their bludgeoning proved more faithful than friends. I became half-blind, an intermittent cripple, groping through pain that pounded with the force of hoof beats in my head. It outshouted my words, outgrew my feet, my small awkward hands. They noticed none of this, diverted by the turbulent shock of my hair, my spectacles' thick lenses and the poor fit of my overcoat.

Idealist

I was desperate to eat at the plain table of the poor
drink the wine of hard labour.
Hunger and thirst drove me in summer
to a farm family who permitted me to live
simply, draw water for the cows
heap up manure with my thin arms
unearth obstinate beetroot.

They offered me black coffee
cream cheese which I refused
craving frugality and bare truth.
When I enquired of their desires, they did not speak
about the earth's abundant beauty, rain
clinging to grape leaves
the moon's translucence.
No one mentioned contentment.

The silence spread a heaviness between us.
I spoke of bloodshed we'd have to endure
in order to overleap the pity
naked in their eyes. At last I realized
my hands were unwashed from the fields
my clothes unclean
my hunger a millstone so immense
no one would beg me to stay.

Lyrics from a *lycée*

1. The classroom

This room my students
inhabit as sparrows
inhabit a cold tree
uneasily
craves warmth and more

light. The little we get
in winter sweeps the wall
mornings, lays a pale hand
on the chalkboard, on definitions
of metaphor

on each bent head. A dull flame
hovers briefly, scatters
a transient glow. I hold my breath
and watch the relentless
fading of each new day.

2. The students

I try to imagine
what's under the skin
what lives inside the slim bodies
the perfect skulls
of these lovely ones.

Something is
straining against flesh
clawing aside veins
and tissue

the way a woman buried alive
might claw away the earth.

Something is beating
like a trapped swallow
against those fine ribs.

It may be exquisite
or something so treacherous
when it breaks through
flesh and skin
reveals tentacles and a fanged mouth
they will be torn
open. They will be helpless
as sheep, their tongues dumb
with terror.

I who have urged them
with my burning words
will find no syllable, no cry
of consolation.

3. The teacher

My child I say
addressing a pupil in my class
you must go early to bed
eat wholesome meat and bread
breathe often of the country air
and take time to play.

I'm sounding so much like my mother
who follows me to unfamiliar towns
wanting to feed and clothe me

with her breath. Her presence
fills the doorway
lingers on windowsills
of each new room. She inhabits
a house completely
making it safe
with the tightly woven texture, steel
bonds of her love.

4. The lesson

I lead my philosophy class
into a stone wilderness
to meet King Lear. The wind
gusts violently as we climb the slope.
Vultures circle silently above us.
I take my students by their soft warm hands
in anticipation of the pain
when the king cries out
My God, my God
why have you forsaken me?

In the falling darkness
someone stumbles. We all come home
with bleeding feet.

Revolution

Restless and discontent with being
a spy, I yearned to stand
openly between two soldiers
a loaded gun in my hand. I was impatient
for Spain, for my red scarf,
for my militia uniform. Someone granted me
reluctant permission to select a gun.

At the river crossing my heart beat rapidly with joy.
The sky was sapphire, everything so still
and beautiful. A silver tingling
at my fingertips. I was terrified beyond all
knowing and prepared for wounds.

Someone discovered my clumsiness
and ordered me to a safe place in the camp
cooking. A pot of boiling oil spilled over
on my leg. It wasn't the wound I wanted.

Nor do I want the memory of a boy
captured carrying a picture
of the Blessed Virgin.
Durruti whom I admired in some respects
forced him to choose at fifteen
within a space of the sun's rising
and setting between revolution
and death.

Two anarchists tell me of killing
one prisoner, a priest,
and letting the other go
free. He turned
and when he had walked ten paces

he was shot. At this the anarchists expected me to laugh.

Interlude

After the Civil War in Spain I turned pacifist
and for a while abandoned politics
for art. In Amsterdam
Rembrandt spoke in sombre tones to the eternal
hunger inside me. I composed poems, dreamed
of rewriting *Electra*, translated the *Iliad*, began
sculpting Justice, her bare unequal arms
holding at uneven levels
equal weights.
I hungered for the absolute
truth of music, beauty of line and colour
the exact texture, pure shape
of love
in the midst of affliction.

Baptism

I refused to let the priest baptize me although my body longed for the bread he held in his hand and my soul thirsted for wine. Grace and unwavering attention kept me in my rightful place outside the gate where smoke of burning nettles seared my nostrils and the stench of charred flesh satisfied for a while all hunger. Congregations of gaunt eyes, the fellowship of bruised and broken limbs surrounded me.

(Fleeing across the sea to Casablanca we were surrounded by water, blue and holy. If we had been torpedoed we would all have been immersed. A more beautiful baptismal font would not be possible.)

Pensées

Someone is leaping and leaping in the air
each time a little higher. This is not
the way to God. Nor can imagination
fill the emptiness, command growth of wings,
defy gravity.

I am waiting for the utter silence before dawn.
I will nor move or weep.
Even desire for grace
may cloud the approaching light
that alone lifts from the heart
all fear.

* * *

From the cross Christ
veiled in the dark
shroud of disbelief
cries out *my God*
my God.

* * *

God exists because I desire him.

Memos to a government in exile

1.
This is to inform you of my vocation for danger, my undeniable calling to suffering and death. I request your permission, your help and your unfettered blessing. Send me to the front, to the fateful centre of the battle which is my rightful place.

I have asked God to make me a cripple, paralyze my arms, thighs, legs. Immobilize my neck and torso. In return I've pledged him absolute attention.

I beg you to send for me soon.

2.
I dream nightly of leading a small band of women into war where the danger is greatest. Where blood pools from wounds gaping in the dust and sun, and the outcry of the dying consumes the sombre light. Where the night is riddled with machinegun fire and fear. Where only the cold rain washes the stiffening corpses.

We will be faultless as doves, tranquil as angels whose wings hold healing. We will wrap ourselves in the skin of a white lion. We will come singing.

This dream is given to me by God. I have carried it in my arms the way one carries an only child: with hunger and love and constant trembling. It is my duty and my desperate joy to lay it before you.

Tacitus tells us we will not be the first. Germanic tribes, nomads of the first century sent virgins into battle, surrounded them with warriors, the bravest and best. Do you imagine it impossible to find in France women with an equal measure of grace? Women with courage in their clasped hands? Believe me when I tell you we will be ready for death.

(I have warned you we will be few. And as I promised, undefiled.)

3.
When we have buried the last dead, scrubbed their blood from our hands, the caked mud and tears from our faces, what then? Then we must believe God, for whom the heart longs, exists a great distance beyond everything we have imagined. Beyond the stars, beyond the expanding universe. Beyond thought. The desire to reach him is a great folly.

We must abandon hope. Turn our backs on consolation.

We can only cry out.

Grief

They've brought me broken beyond mending
into a room silent and pure as a mountain
I remember from childhood. Here
they offer me a cup of egg white whipped with sherry
and a very ripe peach.

They believe I'm dying of hunger, not knowing
hunger is the kind of grief leaves you sterile
as stone
in which no seed can germinate.
Sorrow enters you and you become
the colour of dead leaves.

The greatest grief is knowing what I hold
inside my throbbing head,
what I hunger to offer the world
remains invisible to their blinded eyes.
I want to cry out in rage, force them to probe
each lucent phrase I've spoken, rip open
every syllable, eat every word. Why don't they
seize me violently by my frail shoulders,
grasp my transparent hand in theirs and ask:
Are these things true?

Dirge

What's left is the impenetrable
cloud of unknowing
and the implicit stars. Mystery
not importunity will keep their sharp points veiled.
Larks warble. The beloved wind
blowing where it chooses
shreds clouds into the myriad
fragments of regret. Is it desire
stirs morning grass into an emerald sea?

Who's there to tell us
the afflicted (if attentive
and motionless and mute)
will catch above time's cruel transience
above the swallow's flight
an echo of the absolute? The unmistakable
breath-taking wingbeat of grace.

Heimatlied

Born of a woman

1.
You feel like laughing.
From deep in your belly
this child leaps out
from between your white splayed thighs
like a fish, scales glistening
red-flecked and slippery.

Already you've forgotten
the long wait for her
flawless shaping
to outgrow your own
flesh and blood, the sheltering
darkness inside you. Forgotten
the pain that came like the searing
thrust of sharp lances.

2.
My sister's pregnancies ended
in breech births. All four of them
wanted the womb's moist warmth
and the silence to go on
holding them.

They reached out with their perfect feet
first, as if testing for warmth, or
trying to find a foothold
in time. My sister pushed them out
screaming
with every ounce of strength.

3.
Aunt Emily called to say
Marla gave birth this morning
to twins. Boys. They cried out
in surprise
and breathed, both of them
bravely for whole minutes. Then
as if unwilling to be
small accomplices lured into light
and sound conspiracies
they puffed out their last thin breath
turned resolutely
blue and so silent.

Undercover

I've rehearsed this
repertoire of faces
poised on my dressing table
waiting to be worn. Each one

precisely fashioned to fit
any occasion in life
or death. Gaunt muzzles of bone
bits of fur laced together
feathers and soft leopard skin
the dry shell of a snake.

I assure you recognition is impossible.
I'll charge out of here
and set them quaking with my roar and rattle
teeth bared like swords, or
glide into a gentle evening
of Brahms and conversation
politely sipping wine
never removing these smooth gloves.

When I return to this room
I'll examine each piece for wear
meticulously join torn parts
with needle and thread
recover each frayed edge.
I must let no one
discover my true skin
my fragile flesh, quick breathing.

If anyone touches
the trembling underneath
I am undone.

On guard

Two girls straddle the sawed-off branch of an elm,
a giddy elevation, a vantage point
from where the swollen river's visible:

willows thigh-deep in water, current purposeful
and swift. Red squirrels chase each other
up and down a crooked oak

as if there's no tomorrow. The girls hold tight,
giggling their silly glee, their fear of height.
Below them: an extended family from the Philippines

three deep around a picnic table piled with lunch.
A bunch of men at the barbeque, arguing.
Children break free, head off in all directions,

fleeing mothers, anxious aunts who warn them:
Don't go far!
A kid on a bike zips through the northbound drive

at the crosswalk, properly. A pick-up truck stops short,
the driver through the open window snarling:
What the fuck this stupid crosswalk shit!

Did I mention the dad at the base of the elm,
arms akimbo, head tilted back,
eyes on his two girls out on a limb? Did I say

it's early spring, too soon for tulips?
The immigrant women craving columbine,
anemone, delicate coral bells.

The men around the barbeque brew remedies
for a world gone wrong.
(It's not the truck driver's words that shock

but the utter absence of expression on his face.
The eyes' intention veiled by shades.
The granite calm of sunburnt, grizzled cheeks.
The square, steel jaw.)

Warning to residents

Don't give in
to the old woman
who comes to you with outstretched hands
begging for bread
water

They've taken everything away she says
The shelves are bare

Lead her back
down the narrow passage to her room
Confront her with the evidence
of plenty
in the well-stocked cupboard

Try to make her tell about the apples
and the white rose

Don't be moved
by the terror in her voice
or the dull sadness Remember
her face
her empty bone-thin hands are capable
of great persuasion

October

Yours is a north room. Bed, chest
of drawers, a chair, closet for a few clothes,
uncertain light.

                                        Autumn:
you can watch the last gold zinnias shrivel,
asters diminish in the night frost.
Abandoned leaves weave slow October dances
on dead grass. When the branches are bare
someone lowers the purple martin house
almost to the ground, finally
a clean shroud covers everything.

When the cold closes in,
unfold your thickest afghan, hold your arms
tight to your heart. Warmth
may or may not creep into your breast,
unbind your frozen feet, reach
the blue tip of each stiff finger.

This room where we've brought you
for your own good
is the smallest you've inhabited
so far. It holds the least distractions,
almost no false promises.

                                        Examine the space
here on the calendar, explore corners,
search as often as you like
under the bed
for misplaced treasure, fragments of
lost time, elusive melodies of songs
you were always desperate to recover.

We leave you now to rest
before supper. Close your eyes.
Unclench your fingers. Before we go
we'll cover you, turn off the light,
commend you in a heartfelt prayer, briefly
to God.

It isn't death

It isn't death the woman fears
so much as the steady lessening
of her fragile hold on things:
the pink rose china
in shards on the floor,
elusive patterns of calendars,
names of grandchildren she loves.
Lately she hears only children's voices
faint as a breath, unclear,
their laughter always bordered with fear.
Her fingertips move dull as wood
along walls and tabletops.

She dreams empty streets
in austere cities so far removed
she can't tell how she came there.
Tapping her steel-tipped cane
on stones, she inches along
from one precarious intersection
to the next. When the street dissolves
as usual into mist
or comes to a dead-end
she turns. Retraces her steps.

At noon the cruel sun strikes
at her face.
There are no birds or trees
or people here
and not much light.

It isn't darkness she fears so much
as the shrinking away from her vision
of everything. On a frail horizon

the world recedes. She keeps on
reaching for its pale edge.
No telling how much longer
she can continue
to hope
to breathe.

Heimatlied

The old woman speaks frequently
of going home. She doesn't mean
the white bungalow on some suburban street
she remembers only as long
and thin and light-filled.
She's not referring to the shack
sheltered by green aspen, April rain
dripping through the tar paper
roof. Windows and walls white with frost
by November.

She doesn't even mean the solid brick
house abandoned in the village
Vassilyevka. It floats dreamlike
in her brain, insubstantial, sunlit
as the day she left. All hope,
the horses' heads, the
train's wail aimed north.

Home
is farther off than that.
And nearer. It is neither north
nor south. It is a far country
carried in the heart. The weary
woman dreams of it. The streets,
neither pointed stones nor gold,
hold comfort, like the sweet
remembered stanzas of a song
she sings for you. Her voice is thin
as filament. And breathless.

Stars to steer by

We buried the woman in a frozen portion of the planet
and drove home. The unwilling sun hung low
over Winnipeg. Wind scoured the streets.

She was poorly dressed for the weather. Ungloved hands
at rest for once, feet ice-cold, motionless,
a face as unrevealing as the moon's.

Over tea, grieving, we recited landscapes
where she might have been laid to rest. In waters
of the Dnieper River when the hydro dam blew up,

refugee camp in Yugoslavia, trapped in the Russian zone.
Might have lain with her exiled husband in permafrost,
the blood-flecked snow her shroud.

Trekking west with the retreating German army, lost,
children in tow, she became irresistible.
Dive bombers swooped like vultures

once

          twice

                    again.

She herded her children into a culvert,
shoved her own head after them and waited
in the rusty dark for silence.   Dying

in Winnipeg (a lifetime later) she said
all she ever wanted was her children saved,
a face that could be recognized in death. She wanted,

rising over mud and gunfire,
an uncorrupted moon
and quiet stars to steer by.

New Poems

Where were you when

1.
A dog leapt out of the ditch to snap at me.
I veered to avoid fresh roadkill, pedalled past
a golf course, three empty churches, a closed country store.

On either side the golden glow of aspen leaves.
Above me screaming geese wedged and wheeled
against the flax-blue sky.

As if I'd need them, St. Teresa's words entered my head:
Let nothing disturb you,
nothing frighten you.

At the A&W we praised the perfect autumn day.
The blue and gold. The coffee hot and strong.
I pedalled home and turned the TV on.

What happened on that day is history:
those lethal fires long since doused,
debris swept up, the dead identified
if possible, mourned, buried.
The perpetrators hunted down
and New York reimagined.

2.
My mother and I are drinking tea
in her tiny room. The nurse brings pills.
I turn the TV on, the screen explodes:
chaos at the Kabul airport: tangled arms
reach out for helping hands, feet for foothold.
Mouths gape with horror. A frantic scramble:
rats from a sinking ship.

The nurse says: "It's the Taliban."
My mother, trembling, asks: "What's Taliban?"
I grab the remote. There must be a game show,
talk show, cooking show, something
that won't frighten my mother who is frail,
confused, dead tired. It's getting late.
She should be sleeping.

Dawn: A Triptych

1.
Giotto, in his *Nativity*, has Joseph
hunkered between sheep and donkeys,
grey head lowered, eyes closed.
Above him, radiant as the dawn,
Mary adores the baby she's just born
and in the sky the angels are
beside themselves.

What's troubling Joseph might be fear:
he knows harm hovers over children
of any age, in every age. Bullied in schoolyards,
abandoned in a shopping mall. At the mercy
of a sudden fever, accidental tumble
down a broken stairway, skewed
strategies of fear- and ego-driven tyrants.

He could be contemplating genealogies—
his or hers. Legitimate (or not so)
lineages where a putative father
lines up with kings and refugees
patriarchs and prostitutes
gentiles and Jews.

Of course he's mystified. Who wouldn't be
when eternity invades time? The abstract
enters finite space and settles there
in skin and swaddling clothes, blood
flowing warm and bright through a baby's veins.
Any father would be terrified to think
how easily it spills.

2.
In Edvard Munch's *Golgotha*
Christ hangs
as if suspended from a stretched out cloud
that is the hand of God.

The suffering is over.
Altered by death, his body
is translucent, light as spirit.
All glory gone from his bleached face.

The crowd has seen enough
and turns, as crowds do,
from too much agony or
too much naked love.

Munch, as if weary of painting
utter horror, greed, manic laughter
and anxiety, has left
a host of faces blank. Instead

he's added pigment to the sky,
a hint of brightness round that narrow cloud.
As if he believes, or wants us to:
soon the day will dawn.

3.
It's morning in Giotto's *Resurrection.*
Light shines on the empty tomb, elated angels.
Only the sleeping guards are still in shadow.
The barefoot woman kneeling must be Mary Magdalene
and exiting at stage right, Jesus, in a snow-white robe.

Mary's reaching out with both arms:
She wants to touch, *be* touched. Who wouldn't
want to hold the hand of one so visibly alive?
Who wouldn't be put off when he says:

Noli me tangere

Paused between two acts, one finished and
one imminent, Jesus is leaving Mary
in the garden. Shadows will vanish,
the guards will wake and rub their eyes.
The angels will unfold their wings and fly

and it will dawn on Mary
that she too must rise and run
as she has never run before.
Her feet, swift and beautiful,
will scarcely touch the ground.

Autumn lament

On the last day of September everyone wore orange:
kids in their classrooms, tellers at my bank, bus drivers,
television host.

Leaves fell, yellow and red. From weeds beside the trail
a common sparrow flew up and settled on the branch of a birch.
It was grey, bedraggled, cold.

Every thistle is part of the planet and every moth. Every
pinion and shadow. Even the tiny egg of the cabbage butterfly
and the scruffy coyote who howls a lamentation.

Today's paper carried the names of children in my province
who weren't permitted to grow old. Who were buried
far from their mothers and grandmothers

in unmarked graves. Column after column
marching down the front page and over to the next.
To this enormity, though I wear orange,
I will not be reconciled.

Deliverance

Canada sends Ukraine more ammunition
—WINNIPEG FREE PRESS, 25 MAY 2022

Poisoned air from mutilated industries,
noise of detonations. I cover my ears against
the groan of gunfire, screaming missiles.
At the collapsed bridge I share the terror,
at border crossings join the migrant line.
When I can't bear another blood-stained body
splayed in death, one more blank mother-face,
those cold and hungry children, the remote
rescues me. I write checks, send e-transfers.

War is a hungry beast and we must feed it,
we are told. The means to deliver death will also
deliver peace. Who will deliver from despair
women east and west of Bakhmut who cradle
in their mother-arms the broken bodies
of sons they carried in their bodies, then
with groans of victory delivered.

The City

They confessed that they were strangers
And immigrants on earth
People who say this make clear
That they are looking for a homeland.—HEBREWS 11.13–14

They hold in hope a place
where they will lay their burdens down and sleep
on any old hard floor,
undisturbed by noises in the night,
chokehold of fear.
They've come through far too many dangers:
their feet are wounded, throats parched, garments dirty
and torn. They lead their hungry children by the hand
and when they are interrogated,
confess that they are strangers.

At any moment on this planet
a grave percentage of its more than seven billion
people are on the move. They slog through swamp,
disease-infested jungles, cross treacherous oceans
in flimsy crafts, enter forbidden airspace,
hoping to arrive at haven, shelter, hearth.
A place from which they will not need to flee.
They dream unviolated lives. Are we not all,
no matter where or what our birth,
immigrants on earth?

When the distant sky mirrors
the glow of street lights, travellers look up,
believing they've arrived
at the destination they've long longed for.
A city on a hill. A place of refuge.

But suddenly the streets veer
sharply, lead uphill or down, merge, intersect.
Where least expected there's a dead end.
Terrified, they cry out: Lostness is our greatest fear.
People who say this make it clear
that they are aliens who have not yet found
the city with a firm foundation.
They don't demand a rapid-transit system,
unbroken infrastructure. They've seen systems crumble,
tall towers fall, walls weaken and collapse.
They want someone to hold them by the hand,
someone who knows the narrow pilgrim way
that leads to the eternal city. Someone
who understands
how urgently they're looking for a homeland.

Souvenir

You thought you'd dig up the porcelain cup
your grandmother buried beneath an oak tree
before she turned her back on the apricot orchard
and shut her ear to the nightingale's evening song.

You thought you'd find a red brick
inscribed with your name.
You thought you'd be the one
to bring home hidden manna.

Porcelain shatters easily as hope,
the best bricks crumble,
your grandmother's gone
and what is manna but metaphor?

Windows arched like eyebrows, ornate gateposts,
stairways curving heavenward—are they not
constructs of desire, filtered through time, space
and your imagination?

This wooden bench beside the road—it's real,
and the women who sit here at dusk
with their geese and goats, watching the world
rumble past on a pot-holed road.

Their grief is real too. Not only what they've lost
but what they've never had.
They breathe the evening air and smile at you
and there's your souvenir.

If that is not enough, kneel here
beside the road. Pick up a small white stone,
pretend your name is written on it.

Put it in your pocket.
Bring it home.

Dance of the bald eagles

Day is drained of all but its last light,
sky, a vacant space above the troubled city.
Two shadow-shapes emerge as one and rise
with grace, transcending time and discontent.
Look how they enter the empty stage, circling,
soaring. Their black wings wide, they float
toward each other and converge and then
like interrupted conversation waft apart.

The shadow-dance is not a polka, not a waltz.
Ballet, maybe: a solemn choreography
enacted above blaring horns, crunch of snow
beneath the angry demonstrators' feet.
Day is done, darkness covers outrage.
How gracefully the eagles leave the stage.

Adrift

Pelicans camped on water, a solemn slumber party.
Every shift of an orange pouch, each lifted wing
a signal. On the bridge crossing the river
long white transports heading east, heading west.
What else am I asked to witness? What more
information? A swath of death left by a vehicle
wilfully aimed. Another body left in landfill.
Evidence with too much weight for me to carry.

Ducks in the river sink and surface, a routine
they practice without ceasing. I will rejoice
at the return of water birds, learn to weep
with those whose losses I can't measure,
stay close for comfort like the pelicans
and drift north with the current.

Focus

That dark shape on the opposite riverbank
might be a chunk of mud, a black rock, rotted wood
or who knows what. I turn from what I can't define
to the trio of coots in the foreground. And those
endearing buffleheads—now you see them,
now you don't. Through my binoculars

that thing across the open water acquires
two thin legs. No discernible head.
I focus, hoping it will declare itself.
Maybe the eyes I cannot see stare
into a distant dark side. A quick
shifting of shape

and suddenly a head crowns the crook'd neck.
Appendages so odd they make me laugh
open and extend. Two massive wings,
unfolded, execute one slow preliminary flap,
followed by ungainly lift off. The heron rises
from the riverbank. Not high. Not gracefully.

An orange beak precedes, thin legs follow.
The blue-grey awkward angel
barely skims the water birds
and disappears behind the willows
like a thought not quite thought through.
A concept far too hastily conceived.

First flight

A butterfly, its wings wet,
legs unsteady, wobbles toward me
on the balcony. In June
four gorgeous caterpillars,
emerald, gold, black grew longer,
fatter, feasting on my dill.
Gorged, they wriggled down
the stripped dill stalks
and disappeared.

I knew what they were up to
but not where they went
to fashion waterproof protection
for procreation. Wombs
to hang from something,
somewhere. From there

this newborn at my feet has come
to show me it is beautiful.
Jet black velvet overlaid with glimmering
gold, a tinge of blue.
Has it come to thank me? If so,
where are the other three?
Did I not let them also feed on dill?

Wings dry, legs steady,
(and me as witness
to its maiden flight)
Black Swallowtail lifts off
from the balcony and rises
up, up to the flaming sun.

Epiphany

A coyote leaves the snowy riverbank and lopes
along the street. The sun, a fireball guarded by her dogs,
limps doggedly past winter solstice.
From shrubs beside the 7-Eleven a crow ogles the orb.
It is the season for revelation: something holds me
in its grip, nudges me past lethargy, past in-
convenience, in new directions, east or west.
As if a star in the night sky steers me,

revealing what I've overlooked or never understood:
the need to cast off burdensome possessions,
old grudges, convictions clung to way too long
past due date. Evening comes as slowly as a camel
plodding on sand. In winter's shallow light
crow shivers. The coyote's fur is gold.

Baffled

How high is higher? How wide, how deep is a thought
springing from the divine mind? The path I have chosen
winds past shady poplar, birch, gnarled oak. It is narrow
and leads occasionally past clearings: bluestem grass,
fields of three flower aven, thorns and thistles. Half-hidden
in an aspen tree a pileated woodpecker hammers its heart out.
Chickadees and squirrels vie for seeds hikers have scattered.
A west wind stirs the air, rustles the aspen leaves. Everything
is restless, the prairie sky extravagantly blue, the forest
riddled with light, birds aflutter. The world astir with beauty
I cannot measure. Nor can I count the hordes of refugees
at border crossings, nothing to eat, no water, nowhere to lay their heads,
children kidnapped, abused, abandoned, cities flattened, riots
at football games, another brutal murder in my neighbourhood.
What is God thinking, breathing poetry into the prophet's ear?
Above me a vulture hovers. The wind picks up, trees rattle
their thick branches, rivers swell and overflow their banks.
If there were mountains on the prairie they would roar.

inaugural

a wedding guest lifts cup to lip
and takes a sip of what was ordinary
water, now is wine

everyone is dancing to the music
a woman lifts her hand
and draws a veil across her face

servants are beckoned
stone pitchers tipped and emptied
children in a circle sing

the woman knows what no one else
at this inaugural miracle
imagines

earth convulsed
rocks crumbling
the sun unwilling to shine

she knows the veil
that hides the Holy
will be torn

Advent

We are waiting (again) for the One
who has already come
and gone, leaving us
bereaved.

One waiting in the wings
for the cue: political, apocalyptic
or dramatic—to step into view,
descend,

be finally revealed
to the bewildered crowd—
complicit or without guile.

And to a remnant, impatient

for the curtain to rise on some
anticipated vindication. As if
flamboyant entry to a final act
will finally untangle everything:

a flawless *denouement*. As if
(if you're not left behind)
a book will open up,
page after blinding page.

A rabbi's alleged to have said:
we cannot believe in one for whom—
for reasons philosophical,
emotional or rational—
we do not
(cannot,
will not any longer)
wait.

A brief history of Edison Avenue

When you find it the Promised Land
is a narrow river of mud
that wraps itself like glue around your Russian
boots and bicycle wheels. The fierce sun
grinds it to dust the wind flings
howling in your face. Winters
your children get lost in its white rage.

Trees are enemies you didn't expect.
You must take the axe to their trunks
burn out their everlasting roots.

Evenings you will dream
of the Lost Paradise. Wind breathing
through gold-bright wheatfields,
fragrance of apple orchards in spring.
You will pore over pictures of majestic horses
harnessed to your Sunday carriages, camels,
herds of fat cattle. Such dreaming

must be unlearned.
You must never forget God
brought you here to tend one tethered cow
a small barnful of leghorns
a kitchen garden where the trees grew.

He wants you to love him in a clapboard church
you build when you've made the long way
home from peddling onions eggs your first ripe corn,
speaking politely to English ladies
in River Heights.

Purify your flesh, scrub from it the sweat
of foundries and sewing factories
purge from your soul the street car's jangling.
Join the saints arranged in fixed rows
yearning for worthiness. Listen to the choir

sing (in four-part harmony, in German,
a capella) about carnelian, topaz, dazzling
rubies that adorn the New Jerusalem,
God's shimmering bride beyond the wide
crystal river, its fertile banks moist and cool
in the shade of green cedars
forever.

Aubade

When I awake, the world is waiting
with the scent of fresh-cut grass,
aspen branches tossed by the west wind,
a radio playing *Ode to Joy*.

Neighbours are revving, rushing off to work.
A bird is trying out three notes of a familiar song
and the sun paints a jubilant path across the table.
Coffee's ready and the new day has begun

to inscribe my blood and bones with implication.
My wayward compass is recalibrated:
the needle comes to rest at its magnetic north.

Waging peace

> *How beautiful on the mountains are the feet*
> *of the messenger who announces peace.*—ISAIAH 52.7

Not something separate. Not
a convenient screen, walls hastily thrown up
to keep a conflict's blaze contained.
Or the self safe.

Not something hammered out at tables.
And never sentimental, say a moonlit evening,
incandescent sky or the wide Pacific Ocean
on a breathless night. You might as well

wage peace as war. You'll have to stand
exposed at the crossroads of unguarded anger
a presence, not an absence.
Not gritting your teeth,

not forcing your clenched hands
open. Your heart's timid core
and everything the stubborn mind conceals,
revealed. Disarmed

you become disarming,
the terror in your unmasked face
radiant. Your unshod, wounded feet
beautiful.

AFTERWORD

Networks of Meaning

Sarah Klassen

When I was in grade seven, my family moved from farm to city and I left a crowded one-room country school for a crowded urban classroom. I found a new friend. At day's end, she and I walked home together, holding hands and reciting:

And the night shall be filled with music
And the cares, that infest the day,
Shall fold their tents, like the Arabs
And as silently steal away.

What was it about Longfellow's poem with its imagery of care-infested days and tent-folding Arabs that appealed to two junior high girls? The rhythm and rhyme, of course, but what else gives poetry its power?

While contemplating this afterword, I came upon words by Michael Edwards in *The Paris Review*:

> Poetry attracts our attention to language and to the mystery of words, to their capacity to create, almost by themselves, networks of meaning, unexpected emotions, rhythms and a music for the ear and for the mouth. . . . It burns up appearances, it uncovers the invisible, it opens, like a little casement or a great window, onto the unknown, onto *something else.*

My friend and I weren't conscious of "the mystery of words," nor were we looking for "networks of meanings": reciting poetry gave us pleasure for the moment, nothing more. But maybe, though we didn't know it, we were being prepared to look through the window of poetry for the as yet invisible *something else* that lay ahead of us.

Canadian poet Tim Lilburn describes poetry like this: "Poetry is consciousness dreaming of domicile at the core of the foreign world, the mind deeply homesick and scheming return, the tongue contorting itself toward uttering what such a return might be like" (6).

Poems can reflect back to us this timeless and universal human longing for home, for Eden. In a world where increasing masses of people are on the move, on land, air, or troubled waters, looking for a place of peace and rest, the idea of home shields us from despair.

Prairie poet Anne Szumigalski claims: "if the literary arts can be thought of as a mountain, then poetry is at the very peak . . . [where] you are as near the heavens as you can get while still having your feet on the ground" (209–210).

Poetry as a form for human expression has a long history. Greeks set their narratives in epic poems. Hebrew prophets, when they had something important to proclaim—strong judgment, tender consolation, teaching—said it in poetry:

The people walking in darkness
have seen a great light.
On those living in a pitch-dark land,
light has dawned. (Isaiah 9.2)

St. Paul's letters too contain poetry:

If I speak in tongues of human beings and of angels
but I don't have love,
I'm a clanging gong
or a clashing cymbal. (1 Corinthians 13.1)

Shakespeare, whose plays are poetry, shaped the first conversation between Romeo and Juliet in the form of a perfectly constructed sonnet.

A decades-long road leads from my memory of reciting Longfellow's "The Day is Done" to my first try at writing a poem. That road was paved with reading: stories, novels, Shakespeare, the Bible, *Readers Digest*—anything I could get my hands on. And a still longer road leads to the publication of this "new and selected," a project that says a poet has been writing for a long time and published many volumes of poetry. Such a project compels the poet to reflect on how this all happened. And to ask: Is it important? Is it any good? And does this mark an end?

My journey into writing winds back to the 1980s, when I was teaching English language and literature to high school students. New research in education was drifting north from the US and it concerned the development of writing skills in high school populations. As someone who regularly asked students for written assignments in response to the novels, poetry, and plays we were reading together, I found this research both relevant and interesting.

It had often occurred to me that while I was instructing others how to write, what to write, and then assigning a grade to what they had written, I was not writing anything myself except occasional letters and frequent to-do lists. The new research into the writing process encouraged regular journal writing for high-schoolers. And teachers should write with their students. A novel idea.

If I had not chosen a career that required me to engage with literature—poring over it as I planned how to invite my students to think, speak, and write about it—would I have become a writer?

If my mother had not been a storyteller, would I have become a writer? Her often-repeated story about her family's journey to Yalta in 1918 stirred in me the first desire to write. I wanted to turn the facts of her stories into fiction, a process that, according to literary critic Robert Scholes, serves to preserve the narrative. Why, then, did those stories lead, not to fiction, but to poems that form the core of my first poetry collection, *Journey to Yalta*?

An electric typewriter with a clumsy correcting device sat on my desk and students' assignments awaiting my attention lay all around. The prospect of adding to that scattering of papers the pages of my own writing was not appealing. But what about poetry? A poem could fit on one page. It wouldn't add much to the clutter in my room and might fit into my overcrowded schedule.

A friend invited me to a poetry reading. We stood with others among book stacks in a Winnipeg bookstore and watched Gwendolyn MacEwan emerge from behind a curtain, a scrap of paper in her hand. She began reciting from memory poem after poem from her list. The magic and musicality of her words and her voice held us in thrall. I was drawn in by her bold manner of commanding the elements and demanding magical powers.

> The night is molten rock; we wring
> the blood from stars, the blood from stone.
> Enter me, magus, reduce the world
> to fire, water, breath, gold bone.

I don't remember when I was introduced to the poetry of Margaret Avison, whose work occupies a terrain where intellect, spirit, and compassion meet. The sheer vitality of her work as she explores a dingy corner of Toronto, or the nature of God, or human actions and language, demands the reader's attention.

> Yet you are
> constant and sure,
> the all-lovely, all-men's way
> to that far country.
>
> . . . .
>
> lead through the garden to
> trash, rubble, hill,
> where, the outcast's outcast, you

sound dark's uttermost, strangely light-brimming, until
time be full.

Avison, having understood that poetry-writing could be all-consuming, feared that committing to a Christian faith might mean giving up writing. Instead, faith became the lens through which she observed her world, its inhabitants and language.

During the 1980s, stories reached the west about Irina Ratushinskaya, a Russian poet whose anti-Soviet poems earned her seven years in a hard labour camp and five years in exile. In the labour camp she had no paper and was forbidden to write poems. She composed poems in her head, scratched them on soap with a matchstick, memorized them, and when paper became available, wrote them down. Sustained by strong character and deep faith, she not only survived but kept on writing, about her own fear and suffering, but also about resolve.

Though distant from each other in geography, experience, poetics, and subject matter, both Avison and Ratushinskaya were driven by a need to write, and both brought faith and compassion to their work. Both are among the many poets whose work, besides leaving me surprised and humbled, has enriched my thinking about poetry and the need to write it.

Some poets emerge almost fully formed, like Venus from the sea. Others, like me, look for help. Feeling like an imposter, I registered for a short course on writing poetry. We were all beginners, in awe of the one member who could boast of one poem published in a small literary magazine. We were eager, the instructor kind; five of us from the class formed a writing group, my first. Other writing groups and workshops followed. By the time I enrolled in an evening course on creative writing with Robert Kroetsch, I was less nervous, better able to relax and enjoy my course mates, learn to read their, and my, fledgling writing efforts more critically, with more insight and more helpful critique.

Courses, workshops, writing groups are useful in acquiring and honing skills, exercising the imagination, and providing deadlines. Just as helpful is the encouragement and camaraderie they provide to a novice writer who, with more experience, will rely less and less on such opportunities.

Some time after I started writing poems, I read an anthology of poetry edited by Dennis Lee, *The New Canadian Poets, 1970-1985*. In his introduction, Lee noted that in 1959, three first books of poetry appeared in English Canada; in 1964 there were eight; in 1965, twelve; in 1967 seventeen. And after 1970, the deluge. Accurate accounts, he wrote, could no longer be kept.

This information startled me. Who was I to add to such an outpouring of poetry? By this time I was beginning to submit to journals, but who would read another book of poetry? In the end, I absorbed the statistics as I absorbed rejections from editors of literary magazines and Rilke's cautionary question for poets: ***must** I write?* I continued to write and, as Robert Kroetsch had earlier pointed out, writing becomes a way of life.

When I was working on my first manuscript, poet Anne Szumigalski was writer-in-residence in Winnipeg. Here was a writer whose poems were original, whimsical, wise. Her job was to read and comment on the work of local writers. Nervously I showed her my manuscript. Our conversations were hardly a mentorship, but the encouragement of a poet of her stature made me feel more confident. With her encouragement, I submitted the manuscript for publication.

There has never been a lack of something to write about. Travel opened the world for me. Lithuania with its forests, pagan myths, and struggle for independence; Peru with its ancient architecture, and gold; Palestine/Israel where borders and checkpoints were potent images of human struggle to live together despite differences (and where, as I write, all hell has once again broken out). Besides places, people were raw material for the imagination to sculpt with: I delved into the lives of Leonardo da Vinci, Roberta Bondar, martyrs, my students.

Often, I wrote a series of poems about a person, place, or experience, like photographing a subject from various angles to get a fuller understanding of it. (Think of the four characters asked to describe an elephant.) When it came time to organize a manuscript, such poem sequences didn't always fit neatly with other sequences or with other, alone-standing poems. I've often thought I was too quick to publish my first book, *Journey to Yalta,* where the Yalta poems occupy one third of the book, leaving more ideas and images for related poems in subsequent collections. Should I have followed the tradition of the Canadian long poem—Robert Kroetsch's *Field Notes,* Daphne Marlatt's *How Hug a Stone*—and expanded that first section about the family journey to Yalta into a book-length manuscript?

Only once have I sustained a clear focus in that way and that was in *Simone Weil: Songs of Hunger and Love.* It's also the book that required the most extensive research. I read biographies of Weil, her journals, her posthumously published books, as well as critical responses to her life and work. It was enriching and pleasurable preparation. As I wrote, I kept in mind Gwendolyn MacEwan's *The T.E. Lawrence Poems* as the model for the book I wanted to write.

Without a strong bond with the natural world, could Mary Oliver have written those poems we love her for? I grew up in the boreal forest: scratchy undergrowth, hawks soaring overhead, and the call of the whip-poor-will at night. Violets and wild strawberries in spring; saskatoons and pincherries in summer; icy monochrome in winter. My brother and I explored the mysterious network of paths that laced the bush. Whose feet had made those well-worn paths? Who had chosen the direction? Where did they lead to?

The natural world of air, water, flora, and fauna, so threatened now, has always been a treasure trove of raw material for poetry. It is also a sanctuary, a place of retreat. Parallel to my writing life, I skied, biked, and walked when I could, on familiar or new trails. While my body exercised, my brain had time to spin around the day's tangle of information, frustrations, and problems, spit out the detritus, and leave space for fresh ideas and inspiration. I returned to my work with new energy and sometimes with the solution to problems of metaphor and form. Time away from writing is an essential part of the process.

From where I live now, I can follow the northbound current of a wide, muddy river flanked by trees that, as I write, have turned to gold. Above everything, the vast canopy of a prairie sky. A bald eagle leaves its nest in the towering cottonwood on the opposite riverbank, soars high, hovers over the water, plunges to find food. Diving ducks sink and surface. Will the coyote emerge out of the underbrush? Is that an otter returning to the river after a shore leave, to rejoin the beaver on the opposite bank?

Beyond the small portion of the natural world, I'm given to see there are networks of meaning. And mystery. I'm drawn from desk and laptop to stand at the window and stare. And wait for the poem.

Avison, Margaret. "The Dumbfounding." *Always Now: The Collected Poems, Volume 1*. Porcupine's Quill, 2003.

Edwards, Michael. "The Bible and Poetry." *The Paris Review* 12 June 2023. www.theparisreview.org/blog/2023/06/12/the-bible-and-poetry/

Lee, Dennis, ed. *The New Canadian Poets, 1979-1985*. McClelland & Stewart, 1985.

Lilburn, Tim. *Living in the World as if it Were Home*. Cormorant Books, 1999.

Longfellow, Henry Wadsworth. "The Day is Done." 1845. *The Complete Poetical Works of Henry Wadsworth Longfellow*. Houghton Mifflin, 1902.

MacEwen, Gwendolyn. "Elemental." *Afterworlds*. McClelland & Stewart, 1987.

Szumigalski, Anne. *On Glassy Wings: Poems New and Selected*. Coteau Books, 1997.

ACKNOWLEDGEMENTS AND NOTES

The following are details of the original book publications of Sarah Klassen's poems in Lyrik 1.

***Journey to Yalta* (Turnstone, 1988)**

- Awarded Gerald Lampert Memorial Award for Best First Book from League of Canadian Poets.

Agenda
Born of a woman
Cataract
Collector
Haggai
Hosea
Incarnation
Patriarchs
Pharoah's daughter
Preparation
Small deaths
Treatment
Undercover
Zephania

***Violence and Mercy* (Netherlandic Press, 1991)**

- Shortlisted, Pat Lowther Memorial Award from the League of Canadian Poets for best book of poetry by a woman.
- Shortlisted, McNally Robinson Book of the Year, Manitoba Book Awards.

Advent: Montreal, 1989
And the music
Barvenkovo, 1918
Evidence
Horizon
In the potter's house
Interlake childhood II
Language arts

On the banks of the Nile
Procedure
Remembering

***Borderwatch* (Netherlandic Press, 1993)**

- In the poem "Moving On" the English translations of the two German passages are as follows: "Carried on eagle's wings/into eternity" and "No eye has seen/no ear has heard/no mind has conceived" (1 Corinthians 2.9 NIV)

Colours at the border
Health measures
Heimatlied
It isn't death
Matins II
A matter of language
Moving on
October
Triptych
Warning
Warning to residents

***Dangerous Elements* (Quarry, 1998)**

- Shortlisted, McNally Robinson Book of the Year, Manitoba Book Awards.

Artist and medium
Blue chair
Gospel
Seven-year-old girl in a studio
today

***Simone Weil: Songs of Hunger and Love* (Wolsak and Wynn, 1999)**

- Shortlisted, McNally Robinson Book of the Year, Manitoba Book Awards.

Original notes:

- The author is indebted to the following sources:

  Jacques Cabaud. *Simone Weil: A Fellowship in Love*. Channel Press, 1964.
  Robert Coles. *Simone Weil: A Modern Pilgrimage*. Addison Wesley, 1987.

Gabrielli Fiori. *Simone Weil,* trans. Joseph R. Berrigan. U Georgia Press, 1989.

Simone Petremont. *Simone Weil: A Life.* Pantheon, 1976.

Simone Weil. *Formative Writings, 1929-1941,* ed. and trans. Dorothy Tuck McFarland and Wilhelmine Van Ness. U Massachusetts Press, 1987.

The Simone Weil Reader, ed. George A. Panichas. David McKay Company, 1977.

Simone Weil. *Gravity and Grace,* with an introduction by Gustave Thibon. Octagon, 1981.

Simone Weil. *Gateway to God,* ed. David Raper with Malcolm Muggeridge and Vernon Sproxton. Collins Fontana, 1974.

Adolescence
Baptism
Beginning
Dirge
Grief
Hunger I
Idealist
Interlude
Lyrics from a *lycée*
Memos to a government in exile
Pensées
Revolution

***A Curious Beatitude* (The Muses' Company/J. Gordon Shillingford, 2006)**

- Awarded Canadian Authors Association Award for Poetry.
- Shortlisted, Aqua Books Lansdowne Prize for Poetry, Manitoba Book Awards.
- "Rewinding Time," originally titled "Retrospective," won the National Magazine Gold Award for Poetry, 2000.
- *The Saddest Music in the World* is the title of a 2003 Guy Maddin film.

A curious beatitude
Fiction
Genesis
Letters from Siberia

The night sky
Rewinding time
What the boat carries

***Monstrance* (Turnstone, 2012)**

The author and the publisher of the present book are grateful for the permission granted by Turnstone Press to include poems published in the collection Monstrance.

- Winner, Word Award (Book—Special), Canadian Christian Writing Awards.
- "Guide to the KGB museum" shortlisted, CBC Literary Award.
- Shortlisted, McNally Robinson Book of the Year and Aqua Books Lansdowne Prize for Poetry, Manitoba Book Awards.

Original notes:

- In "Guide to the KGB museum," the line "eternity in pulsing hearts" is a reference to Ecclesiastes 3.11 (NIV). Between the two world wars, the city of Vilnius was considered the Jewish capital of eastern Europe.
- "Stars to steer by" is dedicated to all the women who took part in the Great Trek out of the Soviet Union to the west in the 1940s; the poem alludes to *Going by the Moon and the Stars: Stories of Two Russian Mennonite Women* by Pamela E. Klassen, Wilfrid Laurier University Press, 1994.
- The artist in "The Potter" is Barbara Wiebe.

Guide to the KGB museum
In the garden
In translation
On guard
Pileated woodpecker
Prairieology
The potter
The race
Stars to steer by
Two crows
Waging Peace
What we want

The Tree of Life (Turnstone, 2020)

The author and the publisher of the present book are grateful for the permission granted by Turnstone Press to include poems published in the collection The Tree of Life.

Original notes:

- "Tree" is part of the cycle "Perchance to Dream," shortlisted for the Gwendolyn MacEwen Prize in 2014.
- "Rise and Go" and "Higher" and "And Yet" are part of "Rise and Go," a suite shortlisted for the Ross and Davis Mitchell Prize in 2017.
- In "Rise and Go," the migrant is the patriarch Abraham and the prisoner is Dietrich Bonhoeffer.
- In "Beauty," Westerbork was a transit camp in Holland during WWII. Etty Hillesum volunteered at Westerbork before she was sent to Auschwitz.

Alpha and Omega
And yet
Beauty
Hagar
Higher
Magnificat
Rise and go
Travelling with children Or: Sermon series in a Mennonite church
Tree
Window

Notes for new poems

- "Advent": published in *Poetry as Liturgy*, ed. Margo Swiss, St. Thomas Poetry Series, 2007; republished in *A Century of Poetry: 100 poems for searching the heart*, ed. Rowan Williams, Society for Promoting Christian Knowledge, 2022.
- "Autumn lament": published in *Christian Century*, September 2020.
- "A brief history of Edison Avenue": published in *Acts of Concealment: Mennonite/s Writing in Canada*, ed. Hildi Froese Tiessen and Peter Hinchcliffe, U Waterloo Press, 1992.

- "Baffled": published on D.S. Martin's 55 *Project blog,* 22 July 2014.
- "Dance of the bald eagles": published in *Winnipeg Free Press,* April 2023.
- "Focus": published in *Prairie Fire,* Winter 2021.

INDEX OF POEMS